THE FIRST SETTLER
of LEWES

THE FIRST SETTLER
of LEWES

A History of the Fourth Street Preserve

MICHAEL J. RAWL

THE
History
PRESS

Published by The History Press
Charleston, SC
www.historypress.com

First published 2024

Manufactured in the United States

ISBN 9781467158626

Library of Congress Control Number: 2024941845

Notice: The information in this book is true and complete to the best of our knowledge. It is offered without guarantee on the part of the author or The History Press. The author and The History Press disclaim all liability in connection with the use of this book.

To two amazing Lewes women:

Hazel Brittingham, for preserving its past

Peggy Hastings Rollins, for enabling its future

CONTENTS

CONTENTS

Fourth Street Preserve and relevant streets. *Google.*

PREFACE

Lewes, Delaware, is defined by its land, water and history, permanently bordered on the north by the Great Marsh and on the east by the Delaware Bay and Cape Henlopen State Park. Its compact town center is orderly and colorful, with countless gardens and restored historic homes.

Thirty-five years ago, Lewes was just emerging from its long, quiet slumber as a maritime port, fish products capital and small farming region. In 1990, 2,300 people lived in Lewes, many direct descendants of very old local families. The downtown area with seven churches, three of those African American, was surrounded by farms. Only one community with newer homes had recently been built, just outside the city limits.

Today, more than 11,000 people, mostly retirees, live here: 3,500 in town, the rest in new upscale communities tightly encircling Lewes, where housing for another 7,500 will soon be built. Thousands more are relocating to new homes up to five miles inland. All consider Lewes their home.

Almost all the farmland is gone. Within Lewes's city limits, one thirty-acre wooded parcel remains. When the Greater Lewes Foundation, which I direct, was offered the opportunity to save the Fourth Street Preserve, our board was not yet aware of this parcel's history as the first officially deeded land in Lewes. That deed was assigned on May 25, 1670, by James Stuart, Duke of York, to Helmanias Wiltbanck. Wiltbanck is widely acknowledged as Lewes's first settler. His descendants owned, lived on and farmed the Preserve through five generations.

OWNERS OF THE
FOURTH STREET PRESERVE

THE WILTBANCK FAMILY	1670–1818
Helmanias Wiltbanck	1670–1684
Cornelius Wiltbanck (1)	1684–1689
John & Rebecca Wiltbanck Williams	1689–1704
Reverted to Cornelius Wiltbanck (1)	1704–1724
Hanna Wiltbanck	1724–1727
Isaac Wiltbanck (2)	1728–1769
Cornelius Witbanck (2)	1769–1800
David Wiltbanck	1800–1818

THE WEST FAMILY	1818–1905
Robert West (2)	1818–1833
Lewis West	1833–1857
Robert West (3)	1857–1878
Clementine West	1878–1887
William & Margaret West	1877–1905

THE OTHERS	1905–1956
Capt. William Cottingham	1905–1919
Edgar Ingram	1919–1922
Capt. John Steele Wingate	1922–1944
Isabel D. Jacob	1944–1956

THE ROLLINS FAMILY	1956 –
John Rollins/Rollins Realty	1956–1979
Rollins Investment Co.	1979–2023
Margaret H. Rollins 2014 Trust	2023

Owners of the Fourth Street Preserve, 1670–present. *Ray Daminger.*

Incredibly, both by chance and intent, the original core of the Preserve has remained intact for the past 355 years, through several periods of growth and development, none as dramatic as what is occurring now. Today, the Preserve's original 1,155 feet of frontage behind nine homes on Pilottown Road, above the Lewes-Rehoboth Canal, remains the same width as when it was deeded. So do thirty of the 100 acres of forested land that once swept one mile back to Canary Creek.

This history of the Fourth Street Preserve and of those who owned it focuses on three families who were the principal stewards of this historic property for 312 of the past 355 years: the Wiltbancks, the Wests and the Rollinses.

The arrival in Lewes of the first family, the Wiltbancks, has been recounted in numerous tales. The most popular version has them shipwrecked on the shoals of Cape Henlopen, then floating ashore on a sea chest. Variations include Helms Wiltbanck saving a young girl whose parents drowned while swimming with his prized silver pocket watch in his mouth—or his pocket. Another version has the family surviving a shipwreck, but several years earlier, during their arrival from Holland at the port of New Netherland (New York). For the purposes of this book, we have the Wiltbancks arriving in Lewes in a less dramatic way. The challenges they will face over the next fifteen years will be more than enough for any family to handle.

Chapter 1

THE WILTBANCK FAMILY

HELMS WILTBANCK FINDS HIS *PRA SERVE*

The small wooden boat carrying Lewes's first settler and his family nudged ashore on Hoornkil beach on a spring afternoon in 1663. Rocking gently in the swells behind them was the schooner that had brought them south along the East Coast from New Netherland.

Janneken Wiltbanck sat in the bow, her youngest, Abraham, in her lap. Helmanias, already knee-deep in the cold bay water, lifted out four-year-old Cornelius as a second boat, with their manservant and chests of belongings, came to rest alongside.

Wiltbanck was a stocky Swede, thirty-eight years old, as broad in the chest as a lumberjack. He wiped sea spray from his face and looked inland. There, still to be staked out, were eight hundred acres of land granted to him by the Dutch administrator of New Netherland.

Raggedly dressed soldiers from the nearby West Indies Fort helped stack the Wiltbancks' sea chests onto a two-wheeled cart, then manhandled it across the beach and flats and an earthen dike over a stream to the fort. The rough-built West Indies Fort had been erected in 1658 to facilitate fur trading after the Dutch wrested control of Delaware from the Swedes and "purchased" the land from the native Siconese. It consisted of slanting wooden planks that enclosed a drying and storage area for beaver pelts, a general quarters area and a dwelling for officers. Outside the fort were several small log houses with gardens and a number of Siconese tented huts.

During their first weeks, the gregarious blue-eyed Swede from Holland forged an easy relationship with the fort's young commander, Peter Alrich. He asked the half dozen soldiers to call him Helms "Viltbanck" and his tiny wife, Jane.

The soldiers told Wiltbanck about an earlier Dutch fort once located nearby but destroyed eleven years earlier by local Indians. Wiltbanck was assured the Indians were now peaceful; in fact, trade with the Siconese had just resumed. The natives were a quiet, constant presence around the fort during the day, mostly women and barely clad small children.

Helms began to explore the area. North of the fort was an inlet to the South River, just above the river's choppy exit into the Atlantic Ocean. A wide tidal stream flowed south from the inlet. The soldiers said it was six feet deep and could be traveled by canoe for two hours to a large, shallow pond. It reminded Helms of the Dutch water roads he first saw when he came to Holland from Sweden as a student. Three primitive families squatted farther along the waterway, one family in a shack, two others in wood-reinforced caves dug deep into the bank above the stream.

With Cornelius on his shoulders, Helms walked the well-trod Siconese path along the stream. To their left, across the stream, lay flat, sandy land where salt winds allowed only straggly clumps of sea grass, gnarled trees and blackberry bushes to grow. Beyond that was the sparkling South Bay where their schooner, now departed, had anchored.

To Helms's right, the land sloped up to a thick forest. It was a prime location, midway between the fort and the site proposed for a town. The high woodland provided a vantage point to spot ships entering the bay.

Stretching a mile deep beyond the frontage lay one hundred fertile acres that could be cleared for lumber, then farmed. Shallow ponds of groundwater indicated the presence of fresh water. At its farthest point, the land intersected with a thriving marsh and a wide, deep waterway the soldiers had named Pagan Creek.

No one better understood the value of land and the importance of fresh water than people from the Netherlands. The Dutch term *vild banck*, meaning "wild land above the stream," was in fact the root of Helm's own name.

Wiltbanck looked skyward. The path of the sun formed an east-to-west arc over the property, providing maximum light for long growing seasons. He inhaled deeply. The air was sweetened by the smell of sassafras and brush fires started by the Siconese to flush out game.

Hands on his hips, Helms nodded. Here was the perfect *pra serve* where he would build his new life. It had all that was needed: plentiful game; fowl

Pagan Creek as Helms Wiltbanck may have first seen it. *Deny Howeth.*

whose flocks covered the sky; fish that literally filled the inlets; primeval forests of towering white oak, pine and hickory to build boats and houses; dark, rich soil layered over centuries; and fresh, clean water from perennial underground streams the Dutch called *schuykills.*

Not surprisingly, the prime land coveted by Helms had already been staked out. Dirk Pieters, a soldier who lived with his wife at the fort, had bragged of acquiring a "perfect piece of land" from Abraham Clement, a fur trader. But Pieters's claim was only that.

It would take seven more years for Wiltbanck to obtain a legitimate deed for this parcel. When executed, it would make Helms's *pra serve* Lewes's first officially deeded tract of land.

THE SEARCH FOR UTOPIA

Wiltbanck had been in Hoornkil only a few weeks when the windjammer *Saint Jacob* anchored in the bay after two months at sea, offloading forty-one Mennonite settlers from Holland. The expedition was led by a preacher, Pieter C. Plockhoy, and financed by Amsterdam magistrates in the hopes his colony would create "provision thereby for others to come."

Helms had been expecting them. Plockhoy was related to Jane, from the little Dutch town of Zurich-Zee. More than a year earlier, both he and Helms had been made aware of Hoornkil by one of her brothers, Herman Cornelius, a soldier at the fort in 1660.

Like Helms, who had trained in law, Plockhoy was well educated. He was an intellectual, fluent in English and inspired by his friendships with poets, artists and free thinkers in Holland. Plockhoy's vision was to create a utopian commune of religious freedom, where the work, decisions and rewards would be shared equally by all.

Plockhoy had promised his patroons to recruit a useful group of similarly inspired, skilled craftspeople, but the ragtag crew he was able to assemble in Holland was inspired more by free passage and the one hundred guilders paid to each than by the preacher's vision.

With the Mennonites came badly needed axes, scythes, hoes, seed, muskets and powder, cooking utensils and nails. While Helms failed to share Plockhoy's utopian zeal, he was glad for the supplies and the potential workers his brother-in-law had assembled.

However, the Mennonites were woefully unprepared to care for themselves and provoked scorn among the soldiers and the Siconese. Plockhoy's people tried to settle at two sites, but the best land had been claimed by soldiers and trappers. In time, the group, including Plockhoy, his wife and a blind son, located themselves farther along the stream, near the cave dwellers and where a town would one day be established. They felled trees, burned and removed their stumps to create level ground, built rough shelters and set up sentries. Having missed the growing season, they were an unhappy and uninspired group.

Plockhoy's timing was unfortunate. Less than a year after his arrival at Hoornkil, the British King Charles II and his brother James Stuart, the Duke of York, seized New Netherland from the Dutch without firing a shot. They changed the northern settlement's name to New York and dispatched Sir Robert Carr and two gunboats with 130 troops to the South River region.

The Swedes, under Peter Minuit, first settled in northern Delaware in 1638 and already had a thriving colony there called New Amstel with more than 1,200 European residents and a significant trade presence featuring tobacco, mead from breweries and ten thousand furs each year from the local Natives.

First, Carr seized and looted Fort Casimir after a brief skirmish, killing three Dutch soldiers and capturing ten more. He then sailed one gunboat back to the West Indies Fort at Hoornkil, which had been quickly vacated

Onetime site of Pieter Plockhoy's utopian settlement, now a pocket garden. *Deny Howeth.*

by the Dutch soldiers. Only Alrich and a few fur traders remained, along with Helms and his family.

Carr took charge of the fort then marched to the Mennonite camp and its rough shelters of green pine. Helms, who had just been made justice of the peace and head of fur trading by commander Alrich, watched as the helpless preacher pleaded with the soldiers to spare the colony.

Plockhoy may have expected compassion, but the British monarchy had little use for utopian dreams. Carr ridiculed Plockhoy's plans and, in Carr's own words, destroyed the small settlement to its "very naile." Through this experience, Helms Wiltbanck learned an important political lesson: to be flexible with his allegiances while exercising *geheimzinning*, keeping his cards close to his vest. It was a lesson he never forgot.

Most of Plockhoy's group were mustered aboard ship with their tools as indentured servants to be taken to Virginia with the soldiers from Fort Casimir. A few hid, then stayed to become the small core of early colonists. One story has Pieter Plockhoy remaining in Hoornkil until 1694. Another has him dying there soon after and his wife, Judith, remarrying. A third, the most likely, documents the preacher finding his way to New York, leaving Judith and his blind son behind for Helms and Jane to look after. This corresponds with Plockhoy's documented interest in polygamy and

19

other women. A deed shows he purchased property in New York; he then apparently returned to Holland. Researchers, for generations, may have confused Pieter Plockhoy with his blind son Cornelis, and taken Cornelis's caretaker mother, Judith, for Cornelis's wife.

Ironically, in his quest to create a utopia, Pieter Plockhoy had stumbled upon the real thing. For thousands of years, the Siconese, a tall, gentle and trusting people, had lived fully attuned to nature, enjoying a virtually utopian life with cycles of planting and hunting. It would take the British only one hundred more years to eradicate them from their native land.

After laying claim to the southern colony, the British left Peter Alrich in charge of Hoornkil and then, apart from imposing oppressive taxes, essentially ignored the region for the next six years.

HELMS TAKES CHARGE

Because the earliest colonial settlers had proven unable to support themselves, the Duke of York encouraged well-financed people to immigrate instead, requiring them to build a house and use the land to generate crops, taxation on the sale of which would enrich York. Described by historian Benjamin Freer as "the weakest of the weak family of Stuarts," James had no interest in creating an overall system of fair governance, only in profit.

Overseers like Alrich were installed to appoint local landowners, like Helms, as officials to handle disputes and legal matters and impose taxes. As Helms was the first and most prominent colonist, the years from 1664 to 1670 were productive for him and his family. Helms's leadership would not have been greatly contested, as the permanent residents of the colony in 1667 included just "three Dutchmen and their families, a total of nine men, three women, one of those Harmnnus Wilkbanck [*sic*] that had seated there a few years before," according to a written report of the time.

Using his authority as high sheriff, chief judge and tax collector, Helms continued growing his landholdings, financed by the crop bounties each prior farm produced. His duties as *schout* also required Wiltbanck to "take care the Reformed Christian Religion is maintained without permitting any other (contrary) sects."

Wiltbanck actively encouraged others to settle in Hoornkil by promoting it as being rich with opportunity. Small land grants from Helms and Alrich could be acquired by anyone willing to build a house and work Helms's

Colonial farming by hand. *Adobe Stock.*

farms, hand-hoeing channels for seed and irrigation, watering crops, then using scythe and sickle to reap the harvest.

Growing tobacco was very labor intensive but richly rewarding. Since colonial currency did not exist until the early eighteenth century, exchanges of land and other goods were done through barter or credit. One pound of highly desirable dried and rolled tobacco was deemed equal in value to one English pound.

Although the Duke of York was absent and seemingly disinterested, Lord Baltimore (Cecilius "Cecil" Calvert), operating from "St. Maries" in Maryland, was not. Justifying his actions on the basis of a grant given to him by Charles I in 1632, Calvert began actively contesting Stuart's claim to Hoornkil by awarding unofficial land plats of his own to British settlers. It fell to Wiltbanck, as the *schout* of the small settlement's court, to deal with the eager settlers from Maryland who periodically arrived with Lord Baltimore's claims for Helms's and others' lands in hand.

In February 1669, Alrich also granted Wiltbanck the 150 acres that included the remnants of the West Indies Fort. However, due to the ongoing feud between York and Baltimore, Helms and his fellow settlers still lacked undisputed deeds to their properties.

Helms Secures the Preserve

The Duke of York finally showed renewed interest in Hoornkil in 1670. With the support of his brother the king, he created the first formal records of land ownership, canceling out any grants awarded by Baltimore.

Thus, on May 25, 1670, Helms officially acquired the one hundred acres above the stream he had sought for seven years from the estate of Dirk Pieters, who had apparently died. In a single meeting, the tract was acknowledged by Abraham Clemente as being Pieters's and then sold to Helms, who paid Pieters's widow with three thousand pounds of tobacco and "other goods." Through this deed awarded by the Duke of York, Helms Wiltbanck became the first official landowner in Hoornkil, and his beloved preserve became Lewes's first recorded tract of land.

Today, the Fourth Street Preserve includes the same 1,155 feet of frontage and thirty of the original one hundred acres from the deed acquired by Wiltbanck. It is also the only remaining forested land and open space within the City of Lewes.

DOWN PILOTTOWN ROAD

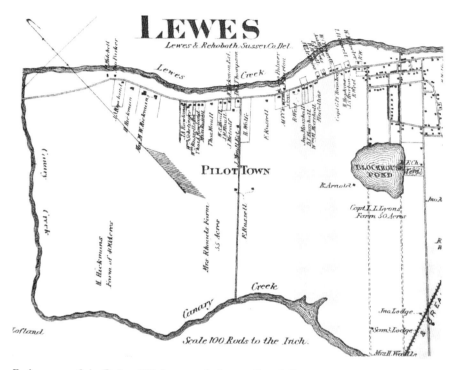

Early survey of the Duke of York patents in Lewes. *From the* Journal of the Lewes Historical Society 5 (2002).

EXPLORING HIS BELOVED PRESERVE, Helm confirmed three slow-moving streams running belowground from Pagan Creek to the canal—three of seven large underground streams in Lewes. Two nineteenth- and twentieth-century maps identify these aquifers with the wording "clear water." One stream branched off to the far right, where it was tapped by Helms on bank land above the stream and became one of the two primary wellheads used by the colonists. Another flowed down the center of the preserve, providing an unending supply of fresh water for farming and for the house Helms built there. The third slanted toward the far left corner of the property.

After the preserve was cleared of trees, tobacco grew well there thanks to the nutrient-packed soil. Water could be tapped and channeled to crops by simply driving hollow pipes into the ground to create primitive artesian wells. The soil was so rich that more tender plants like rye and wheat

A CONFIRMATION GRAUNTED TO DIRCK PIETERS FOR A CERTAINE PIECE OF LAND AT DELAWARE.

FRANCIS LOVELACE ESQR. &C. WHEREAS THERE IS A CERTAINE PIECE OF LAND AT DELAWARE LYEING AND BEING AT YE WHORE KILL STRIKING ALONGST YE KILL IN BREADTH NORTHWEST AND BY WEST ONE HUNDRED AND FIVE ROD DUTCH MEASURE THEN IN LENGTH GOES INTO YE BUSH OR WOODLAND EAST, AND WEST BY SOUTH ABOUT A MYLE ON EACH SYDE WITH A BOWERY THEREUNTO BELONGING AND A KILL BEHYNDE IT ABOUT AN ENGLISH MYLE HAVEING ON YE SOUTH SYDE ANTHONY PIETERS, AND ON YE NORTH WEST SYDE WM. CLAESENS LAND WHERE HE HAS PLANTED BETWEENE TWO BOWERYS WHICH SD PIECE OF LAND HATH BEEN FOR A VALUEBLE CONSIDERACON TRANSPORTED AND MADE OVER BY ABRAHAM CLEMENTIE UNTO DIRCK PIETERS IN WHOSE TENURE OR OCCUPATIO IT NOW IS. NOW FOR A CONFIRMACON UNTO HIM YE SD DIRCK PIETERS &C. YE QUITT RENT 2 BUSHELLS. YE PATTENT IS DATED YE 25TH OF MAY 1670.

fo. 40

Official 1670 deed transferring the Preserve to Helmanias Wiltbank via the estate of Dirk Pieters. *From the* Duke of York Records 1646–1679.

Aerial view of the Fourth Street Preserve today. *Greater Lewes Foundation.*

This original well site provided fresh water from the Preserve to Hoornkil's early settlers. *Deny Howeth.*

would not grow until tobacco crops had reduced the level of nutrients. This encouraged natural crop rotation, since tobacco grew best in fields that had not yet been cultivated. Conversely, if tobacco was grown at one field too long, the soil would become depleted.

Helms and his sons constructed another well near their house by digging down six feet in a wide circle, reinforcing the walls with rock, then excavating more dirt until water was found. While a typical well might require eighteen feet of digging, after only eight or so feet, their new well provided "clear water" for the family and for Helms's growing herds of livestock: cows, pigs, hogs and sheep.

Though he had resigned as *schout* from 1664 to 1667 due to an injury that caused his left leg to be permanently lame (by one report, it was amputated), Helms remained the undisputed master of Hoornkil.

THE ARRIVAL OF DR. RHOADS

Alrich awarded Helms the position of high sheriff again in 1669. One year later, Dr. John Rhoads arrived from Annapolis with his wife, five children and a Duke of York grant for hundreds of acres, including farmland on Rehoboth Bay, where he settled.

Rhoads and Wiltbanck had both brought their families from Europe to pursue opportunities in a new land. They were both major landowners of the same age (forty-six), well-educated and from prosperous backgrounds. But instead of friends, the two men quickly became enemies, with Rhoads bitterly resentful over how Wiltbanck had used his influence to expand his holdings. Also, Helms never fully mastered the King's English. Enough of his Dutch and Swedish words were similar to English that he was able to make do, which could well have offended the elitist Rhoads.

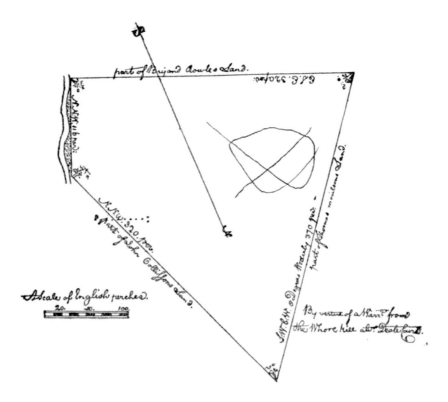

A 1680 survey by Cornelius Verhhoofe confirming Wiltbanck's ownership of Hopewell. *From the* Duke of York Records 1646–1679.

All that remains of Tower Hill: hundreds of new homes and two historic markers. *Deny Howeth.*

A local election soon made both Rhoads and Wiltbanck magistrates of Hoornkil's four-man court. A doctor was a valuable asset for the small colony. For the first time, Helms faced a serious challenge to his sole authority over the colony.

By then, the Wiltbancks had been living in their new Swedish log house at the Preserve, where Helms also conducted hearings of the Hoornkil court. Cornelius was eleven and Abraham eight. In 1671, Helms and Jane had a daughter, Rebecca; a third son, Isaac, was born in 1672.

A 1671 census required of Wiltbanck by his New York overseers recorded a population of forty-seven, including eighteen British (bolstered by the Rhoads family's arrival) and twenty-nine Dutch, plus five men on boats. None of the colony's slaves, of whom there were a growing number; its indentured servants; or the Siconese Indians who frequented the settlement were counted.

Despite the two men's differences, the wives and children of the Rhoads and Wiltbanck families inevitably became close due to the interdependence required of a small settlement. In years to come, marriages between the two families would forge even tighter bonds.

Though he had been farming it for years, Wiltbanck's original eight-hundred-acre claim, Hopewell, wasn't officially certified until 1671 by New York's Governor Lovelace as belonging to Helms and his sons. The deed noted, "Wiltbanck stands possest of a certaynee parcel of land at ye Whorekill in Delaware Bay, part of which he hath maneured (i.e., cultivated)." Hopewell would finally be formally surveyed in 1680.

Across from Hopewell, Helms also acquired 134 acres of a property known as Tower Hill. There, prominent descendants of his youngest son, Isaac, would eventually make their homes and, between 1792 and 1850, be buried in a cemetery just inside the boundary of Hopewell.

There was no road between the properties, as there is today, until the mid-nineteenth century. Although they were big believers in fences, the Dutch were not road builders, preferring instead to acquire land not too far inland for tenants to farm.

BALTIMORE VERSUS YORK: HELMS IN THE CROSSHAIRS

The quarrel over Hoornkil between Lord Baltimore and the Duke of York heated up in late 1671. Acting as a spy for Lord Baltimore, a landowner near Tower Hill reported Wiltbanck's steady acquisition of land to York's rival. At Calvert's direction, the "violent and uncontrollable" Commander Thomas Jones crossed the Chesapeake to Hoornkil with orders to arrest Wiltbanck, confiscate all his land and bring him back to St. Maries, Maryland, to be imprisoned.

An overseer, Francis Jenkins, was also sent to Hoornkil by Lord Baltimore to reassign land grants to Hoornkil properties, including Helms's, to absent Marylanders. Jenkins himself was "awarded" 1,629 acres. Though never enforced, this only created more insecurity.

Jones fell on Helms at the Preserve, put him in shackles and plundered the family's new home while Jane and the children stood helplessly by. Helms's only option was to publicly pledge allegiance to Baltimore, then bribe his captor to allow him to escape while en route to St. Maries.

Upon Helms's return, Dr. John Rhoads was quick to step forward, deviously accusing Helms of treason to the Duke of York because of his recent pledge to Baltimore. This was not a spurious accusation— if convicted, Helms would be hanged, drawn and quartered. He was imprisoned for several days by Rhoads.

Helms's trial for treason took place quickly. Since Helms and Rhoads were justices, it fell to the other three—Smith, Molliston and Southern—to try him. Helms was acquitted to both "cheers and boos" from the assembled settlers.

THEN, IN 1672, EVERYTHING CHANGED

Away from the colonies, the Anglo-Dutch war for the seas and their trade routes continued. While the British had controlled New York for eight years, they had literally let their guard down. Without warning, a massive fleet of Dutch ships carrying 1,600 soldiers overwhelmed the Duke of York's forces in New York. After this fleet seized control of the city, a smaller force sailed south to the colonies.

The Dutch invasion had been well planned. Seemingly overnight, new laws were imposed and the territory renamed New Netherland. Hoornkil was christened New Deale, and earlier York land grants were validated for any settlers who now pledged themselves to Holland. Alrich and the settlers quickly declared allegiance to the Dutch in order to save their homes and farms. Wiltbanck, Rhoads and two others were confirmed again as magistrates.

Half of the ancient boundary stone from 1672 (not 1723). *Deny Howeth.*

The entire town area, already roughly sketched out by Wiltbanck, was officially surveyed by a Dutchman, Cornelius Verhoofe. In 1672, he placed a four-foot-high boundary stone at a site that would become the corner of Shipcarpenter Street and Pilottown Road. Remarkably, that stone remained intact for 277 years until, in 1949, it was broken in half by a truck turning the corner too sharply. One fragment remains on the front lawn at nearby 242 Second Street; another is at 116 Dewey Avenue.

Verhoofe designed the new town with Dutch efficiency. House lots were close together, long and narrow, enabling privies to be placed as far from each home as possible. Green space for trees and gardens was allocated to every house. Walking paths with planting areas for trees were laid out along each narrow street.

THE BURNING OF HOORNKIL

By late 1673, Dutch troops had departed New Deale, and Lord Baltimore launched a plan to brutally punish the town's residents for their frequently changing allegiances.

Three weeks before Christmas, Captain Thomas Howell came to New Deale, purportedly on behalf of the new Lord Baltimore and Maryland governor Charles Calvert, to "protect the settlement from the Dutch." Howell and his forty troops lived off the meager supplies of the community for eighteen days, then briefly left.

On Christmas Eve, Howell returned with his heavily armed horsemen. They assembled the forty-seven men, women and children of Hoornkil by the stream, confiscated their weapons and tortured one settler, Haraman Conelison, to reveal where he had hidden a store of beaver pelts. Then, one by one, Howell's troops burned their eleven homes to the ground, including Wiltbancks's at the Preserve and that of his neighbor, Sam Rusell. Only a single thatch barn near the inlet, used to store wheat, failed to catch fire and was spared. All the settlers' sloops and barques along the canal were destroyed, and any farm animals Howell could catch were seized. The colony's fields of winter wheat and stacks of corn were torched.

Howell, then made aware of the Rhoadses' property, drove his troops three miles down the coast to the farm in Rehoboth, with its house, seventy-foot-long tobacco shed and milk hut. Rhoads and his family were given fifteen minutes before it and the other buildings were set afire. The soldiers even torched the inside of their home to hasten its burning. In Helms's own words, "They burned and left us in unbearable conditions....Neighboring red men wept when they saw the spile [*sic*] what the inhabitants had suffered by their own countrymen."

When Howell's troops departed, the villagers surveyed the damage. All the homes and their contents had been destroyed. The wheat fields were blackened and smoking. The men had no weapons for hunting and no boats from which to fish. In the bitter cold of winter, the community's first need was for warmth. Bonfires were lit, and women and young children sheltered in the barn as the men salvaged supplies.

John Rhoads declared he would make a heroic trek to seek supplies. His choices were to go inland, to Maryland, through friendly Nanticoke country, or upriver to Fort Casimir through land frequented by the hostile Minqua Indians, who prowled the South River by canoes to conduct raids and terrorize the Siconese. Both settlements were sixty miles away. Since help could be delivered more quickly by boat, Rhoads and a fellow settler, Thomas Tilley, decided to go north, without any weapons, hoping to return with supplies within several weeks.

Helms remained with the exhausted, famished settlers. A number of the women were "with child" and unable to travel. Others left Hoornkil altogether. For those Dutch who stayed, their famed perseverance would be

House today on the Pilottown Road site of Helms Wiltbanck's second home. *Deny Howeth.*

31

Restored Swedish smokehouse built by Helms Wiltbanck. *Deny Howeth.*

fully tested. After many days with no sign of help, a trapper arrived on foot with the tragic news that Rhoads and Tilley had been ambushed and killed by the Minquas on their route upriver. They had never reached Fort Casimir.

Helms was now forty-seven years old. His family included two sons, twelve and ten, plus a two-year-old daughter and an infant son, Isaac. He had already acquired well over one thousand acres of land. Although dejected and physically handicapped, his only option was to stay and start over again.

As a first step, Helms decided to not rebuild his home at the Preserve. It had become difficult to walk from there to the expanding town area on his bad leg. So, in 1673, Helms built a new house adjacent to the boundary stone laid by Verhoofe, near the house of Plockhoy's son, Cornelis, and his mother. Years later, Shipcarpenter Street would be laid at the boundary line between the two homes.

Helms's second house remained in the Wiltbanck family through 1900, when a map identified it as belonging to "Squire Wiltbanck." Soon after, it was acquired by the Enos family, then finally razed in the 1930s. A small Swedish plank building Helms built behind his home as a smokehouse can be found today on the grounds of the Lewes Historical Society.

STABILITY AT LAST

When the Anglo-Dutch war ended after less than a year, the Dutch ceded control of Delaware again to Britain. Political uncertainty continued until the Dutch fully withdrew and the Duke of York resumed control of the original territories in November 1674.

In Hoornkil, all prior land patents were fully restored (again) and a proper British court was put in place, with Wiltbanck (again) as one of the five justices. Peter Alrich, however, was finally removed as chief overseer as punishment for assisting the Dutch during their brief takeover. Cornelius Verhoofe remained in Lewes as its surveyor, one of the town's early shipbuilders and a close friend of Helms's. Still more new land grants were awarded to Wiltbanck, including one for the rest of the land between the Preserve, where Helms continued to farm, and the town boundary line by his new home.

The years after 1674 brought relative calm and growth. Helms focused on currying favor with Pennsylvania's new territorial governor, Edmund Andross. Witness a paragraph from one letter Helms sent:

> *The Lord Baltimore thus ar imagine to have this pleats again Lickewise her is ayly severale pesons comin out Virginia which brings news that the rebellion thus continue sill against their gouverneur...and lick to be wors which is a great disheartening to all payes and sober meyndeth people.*

In return, Andross described Wiltbanck as a "man of much intelligence and of great observation and a zealous, public-spirited citizen." He was also one who owned enough land to pay his taxes while collecting the same from others.

Still voracious in his pursuit of property, Helms became even more aggressive, surveying with Verhoofe to claim new tracts and filing frequent lawsuits to protect his assets within and around the town. *The Duke of York Records*, found in the Kent County Recorder of Deeds Office during the Revolutionary War, detail six land transactions, hand drawn by Verhoofe and signed by Wiltbanck, totaling more than 2,500 acres.

Helms even tried to acquire the new town itself. After his utopian colony had been wiped out years before, Pieter Plockhoy had given Helms a written claim to the land he had briefly appropriated. Using the lot plan Verhoofe had laid out, Helms was emboldened to use Plockhoy's document to claim ownership of the town and sell its lots, but his ploy was quickly denied by Andross.

Helms also continued to lobby and adjudicate against the land claims of new settlers who were still being sent from Maryland by the persistent Lord Baltimore. In 1677, Helms wrote to Governor Andross of steps he had taken to encourage a Major John West to leave Virginia and settle just north of Cape Henlopen. "Otherwise," Helms wrote, "it is lickly to be settled by them of Maryland these winter as far as I can unnerstand." He also complained of the "lameness of my one leg," which restricted his ability to travel.

Shipbuilding was by then taking place in earnest on the canal-front land across from Helms's new home. A petition by a John Redwood to build a house there was denied by town commissioners "for there is to be A street (Shipcarpenter) goe up between the blind mans (Plockhoy's son) and Halmanus and may be hinderance for the future buildings of vessels in that place."

Boatbuilding continued in Lewes until 1866, when the region's seemingly unlimited resources of cedar and pine were finally depleted. At that point, shipbuilding moved inland to Milton and Milford and up the East Coast to Maine.

WILLIAM PENN AND THE SECRET PAPERS

In 1681, King Charles II assigned ownership of the forty thousand square miles that would become Pennsylvania to the thirty-seven-year-old William Penn as repayment for a fifteen-thousand-pound debt Charles owed Penn's father, Admiral Sir William Penn. Commander of the King's Navy, the admiral was also a close friend of James Stuart, the Duke of York. The younger Penn hoped to create a new community of religious freedom for the Quakers—a religion to which he belonged—and other sects.

To avoid being landlocked, Penn pressured James Stuart, his father's friend, to grant him the three southern counties of Delaware and thus provide an outlet to the sea. This arrangement included ten thousand acres in Sussex County to be set aside for York and ten thousand more for Penn himself. With his interests turning to Britain, where he would eventually be made king (despite being Catholic), the Duke of York complied.

Penn quickly renamed Hoornkil Lewes and the surrounding territory Sussex, both after regions in his homeland. Five years later, when Charles II died unexpectedly, his brother ascended to the throne as James I, king of England.

Seven Lewes landowners traveled to greet and pledge allegiance to William Penn on the new proprietor's arrival and investiture at New Castle

William Penn. *Adobe Stock.*

(formerly New Amstel) in 1682. Helms's bad leg may have kept him from attending, but Penn was well aware of him.

In May 1683, Penn made a secret five-day visit to Lewes during which he met with Helms Wiltbanck and Haraman Cornelison to gather their depositions, including details about the original colonization by the Dutch in 1631. Both men signed a statement regarding the brutal burning and pillaging of Hoornkil by Howell in 1673. Those papers, known as the Zwaanendale Documents, would be critical to ensuring Penn's ownership of Delaware over a future Lord Baltimore.

Penn naturalized Helms, Cornelis Plockhoy, Cornelius Verhoofe and four others and assigned Wiltbanck as a judge of Sussex County. He also approved five thousand pounds of tobacco to be paid to build a two-story wooden courthouse on land where the first St. Peter's church, a wooden structure, would be erected in 1722.

The number of recorded landowners in Lewes and Sussex County grew after Penn instituted fair trials and freedom of religion through his Frame of Government in 1683 and Charter of Privileges in 1701. These created a powerful legislature in Philadelphia in the English tradition to oversee all Penn's new lands, including the three Delaware counties. Laws and strict penalties were enacted to punish people who cursed, committed adultery or even spoke negatively of one another. Penn also introduced a postal system. In the new Sussex County, the most reliable carriers continued to be members of the Siconese tribe. There would not be a Lewes post office, however, until 1803.

William Penn returned to London for a 1685 appearance before King James II and the Lords of Trade to resolve the Lord Baltimore issue. There, the Zwaanendale Documents and a 1629 deed executed with the Siconese that Penn had found in New York were used to prove a Dutch colony had existed at Hoornkil one year prior to Lord Baltimore's claim.

The king and lords ruled that the "land known as De La Ware" belonged to Pennsylvania, though no other official action was taken. Then, in 1688, Penn lost his patron when King James was dethroned by his own daughter, Mary, and her husband, William of Orange from Holland, who seized the crown in the "glorious revolution." The couple served as co-rulers until Mary's death in 1694. A year earlier, William and Mary had founded a college in Virginia in their names.

Penn returned to Philadelphia for one year in 1700. Despite significant immigration, largely by Quakers, the city had not yet become profitable; instead, for a time, it was more a poorly run haven for pirates. Penn also discovered that the son he had left in charge had become a spendthrift and a playboy. Back in England, a victim of extortion by his financial advisor, William Penn became penniless and suffered a stroke that left him mentally incapacitated. He died in England six years later in 1718 at age seventy-three.

The official determination of Pennsylvania's ownership of Delaware finally occurred through a British court ruling in 1750. An agreement between Penn's heirs and the fifth Lord Baltimore resulted in a survey being done by Englishmen Charles Mason and Jeremiah Dixon, creating both the Mason-Dixon Line, which vertically divides Maryland from Delaware, and the Delmarva Peninsula. Stone markers from their survey work can still be found in farmland and along roads in western Sussex.

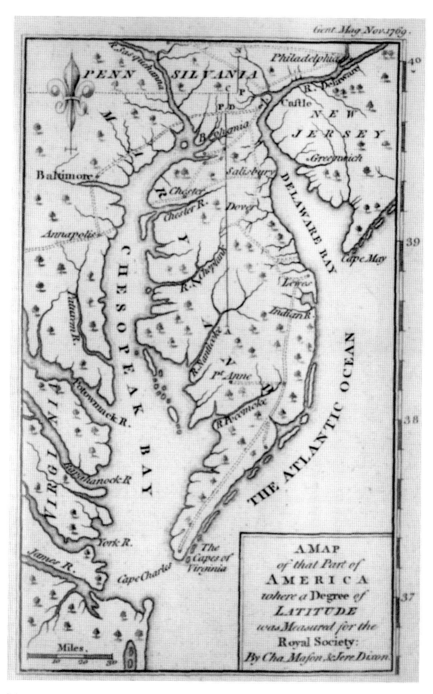

The 1678 survey by Charles Mason and Jeremiah Dixon. *From* Gentlemen's Magazine, *London, November 1769.*

THE DEATH OF HELMS WILTBANCK

In 1683, soon after serving as the executor for his late friend Cornelius Verhoofe's estate, Helms Wiltbanck suffered a severe stroke. On January 15, 1684, William Clark, a fellow justice of the Sussex County Court, wrote to William Penn:

> *Halmainus Wiltbanck on a sudden taken speechless and have no use of his right side, hand nor foot, and have layen soe ever since the last seventh day two weeks, not likely to live long.*
> *Ps—since my writing Halmainus Wiltbanck departed this life.*

Helms died a respected pillar of the community and the original settler of Lewes. The wily Wiltbanck had made the most of his twenty years in Hoornkil.

In his will, Helms left 50 percent of his extensive 3,500-acre holdings to his eldest son, Cornelius, and 25 percent each to Abraham and Isaac. Accordingly, Cornelius would have received 1,750 acres and Abraham and Isaac 875 each. A court was assigned to apportion the land, and the Preserve was included in Cornelius's holdings, with Isaac receiving the 140 acres south of the Preserve adjacent to the town plus 134 acres at Tower Hill. Other larger holdings, like Hopewell, were shared among the three sons.

Jane remarried a local farmer, Thomas Hodgkins, six months after Helms's death. Her decision was prompted by her need for a husband to collect the numerous debts still owed Helms, which the court would have dismissed had she not presented an inventory and brought action.

Hodgkins quickly undertook this assignment and carried it out until his own passing three years later in 1687. Their first suit was filed against the estate of Cornelius Verhoofe for 7,592 pounds of tobacco and 387 guilders. Another of Jane's claims was for a cow and a calf named Brownie. Though the court ruled against this particular claim, the animals "found their way home" soon afterward, and Hodgkins gave Brownie to Rebecca, his new stepdaughter.

Cornelius Wiltbanck was quick to challenge a part of his mother's inheritance, taking her to court over a house and lot in town "next to the blind man," Plockhoy's son, which he was awarded.

Janneken clearly had a falling out with her son Cornelius. Her own will reads: "[To] my dearly beloved Rebecca," clothing, "To my dutiful and obedient and no less dearly beloved sons, Abraham and Isaac, the bulk of my holdings" and "to my son Cornelius," simply—six shillings.

When Jane died in 1693, she asked to be buried with Helms at the "ancient cemetery" where they had attended services. However, the site of their graves remains unknown. The last recorded visit to their graveyard was by Helms's descendants, likely led by Isaac's grandson Cornelius (4),* in 1842, who found markers of etched stone with the name "Wiltbanck" still legible, in the "lower right-hand corner" of the lot.

Cornelius Wiltbanck Comes of Age

By the age of twenty, Cornelius was managing his first farm, acquired from his future stepfather, Thomas Hodgkins. After Helms's death, Cornelius picked up where his father had left off, acquiring and developing numerous interests in both the coastal and inland portions of the Broadkill Hundreds, so named because each parcel could supposedly provide enough resources to support one hundred soldiers and their families.

Around 1692, Cornelius married Jane Maud, a Quaker like Penn and a childless four-time widow. The two held Quaker gatherings at their home, and they formed an equal business partnership, highly unusual for a man and wife at that time. In 1695, they successfully petitioned the local court for approval to construct a grain mill on the Broadkill River where they were adding to their landholdings. The river ran from Milton to the South River (today Roosevelt) inlet. Between 1701 and 1720, Cornelius and Jane acquired more than one thousand acres of land, including town lots in Lewes and two plantations: one, Cain, just north of the Broadkill, and the other, Forrest, at the mouth of the Nanticoke. They also sold 413 acres of Hopewell to John Dunavan, a Lewes carpenter, which represented Cornelius's share of the original 800-acre property.

The decision made by a number of wealthy families to live outside town was likely driven in part by their desire for safety from raids by pirates. Those raids on coastal Delaware towns went on for nearly one hundred years, beginning in 1698 when fifty French privateers plundered every house in town and killed all the livestock, and continuing until 1793. The town's first Anglican minister, William Black, fled Lewes in 1708 after only

---

* To differentiate between Wiltbanck descendants with the same names, numbers are used to denote family generations.

39

a few months following an attack by "Monnsr. LeCroix" with 120 men. "We lying on the very Capes become a prey to every Enemy that comes our way," he explained to his sponsors.

Cornelius's brothers, Isaac and Abraham, still lived with their families on the parcels of land adjoining the Preserve, though Isaac would soon relocate to Tower Hill. Abraham became a Lewes constable and justice of the peace and enjoyed a long and quiet life. He and his wife, Anne, had two sons, Abraham (2) and Jacob. Isaac pursued the same path as Cornelius, using his inheritance to add to his landholdings until he suffered an early death.

Isaac and Abraham (1) arranged for two young boys, William and Caleb Butler, ages seven and nine, to be brought into their homes as indentured apprentices, where they would receive "meat, drink, Washing, Lodging and Apparell" until they were twenty-one in return for working on their "masters'" farms. When released, each boy would be given "a Suit of Apparell from top to toe."

Of particular note, in 1704, Isaac also acquired a three-year-old slave named Prince, who was bound over for fifteen years from his brother-in-law, John Williams.

DARK CLOUD OVER THE PRESERVE

Helms and Janneken's daughter, Rebecca, like most women of her time, was not accorded significant bequests or privileges. When she was seventeen, Rebecca married John Williams. Two years later, in 1689, Cornelius gave her husband the Preserve, adjacent to Rebecca's brothers' properties.

Janneken's will was settled in 1693, leaving Rebecca only "certain wearing apparel." Soon after, that same year, Rebecca physically assaulted Cornelius's wife, Jane, who had her arrested. Rebecca was spared a trial when prosecutors declined to appear in court. Then, in 1704, Rebecca died suddenly at age thirty-three, after which her husband, John Williams, hanged himself. They left behind two young children, a daughter and a son.

There are so many unanswered questions. The attack on Jane occurred soon after Rebecca's mother died. Did Jane provoke it? Perhaps Rebecca had a jealous temper or mental health problems. What terrible circumstance led to both her and John's deaths, and how did that relate to John releasing the young slave Prince to his neighbor and brother-in-law, Abraham, just prior to their deaths? What steps did John take to protect his own young children?

Cornelius quickly had John Williams declared as having been *non compos mentis*, which enabled Cornelius to administer his estate and regain ownership of the Preserve. Then, in 1706, he represented Rebecca's son, John Williams Jr., in court to preserve his rights to the remaining family assets, primarily a four-acre tract in town that Williams had purchased, the deed for which had not yet been transferred from the seller. Soon after, Cornelius arranged to have the young boy apprenticed to Samuel Carpenter in Philadelphia.

While in London years before, the wealthy Carpenter (1671–1714) had become close to William Penn, a fellow Quaker. As one of the earliest Philadelphia settlers, Carpenter used his wealth to acquire enormous amounts of property, including five thousand acres he bought from Penn. Late in life, he became lieutenant governor of Pennsylvania.

This adds to the confusion surrounding Rebecca and John's children. Cornelius was a committed family man. Did he send his young nephew away to spare him unwanted attention in their small community after a traumatic period? Who took care of Rebecca's namesake daughter? Also, how was Cornelius able to approach Samuel Carpenter, the wealthiest merchant in Philadelphia, and why would Carpenter agree to accept young John Williams as an apprentice?

The answers may lie in Carpenter's own past. When Samuel Carpenter was twenty-one, his father, John, sheriff of Horsham, was murdered by his second wife, Sarah. This led Samuel to embrace the Quaker religion, which Cornelius and Jane shared, and relocate to Pennsylvania.

Carpenter and Cornelius likely met in Philadelphia as a result of Cornelius's increasing political activity. If so, it is possible Cornelius knew of Carpenter's dramatic family history and felt he might be sympathetic to young John's situation. All this is, of course, only supposition.

Cornelius was first elected a representative from Sussex County to the new Pennsylvania Assembly in 1698. In 1704, he helped lead a successful petition for Delaware to elect an assembly of its own, due to insufficient representation given the three counties, in particular Kent and Sussex.

The legislators formed "The Delaware State formerly styled The Government of the Counties of New Castle, Kent and Sussex, Upon Delaware." Though Delaware was still under the control of the Pennsylvania governor, this provided a level of freedom that laid the groundwork for Delaware to declare independence on June 15, 1776—the first colony to do so.

Sometime following this period, Jane left Cornelius and Lewes to live in Pennsylvania. She died there in 1718 at age forty-nine. Three years later,

Cornelius married a young widow, Hannah Kollock, of Lewes, who was thirty years his junior. She gave birth to his only child, a son, Isaac (2), in 1721.

On Cornelius's death in December 1724, his entire estate, including the Preserve and his slaves, was left to Hannah and Isaac, then age four. Isaac was specifically given "my negro boy named James to be possest and enjoyed by him and his heirs forever."

Hannah remarried a Mr. Broddy but died herself in 1727 at age twenty-nine, leaving Isaac a ward of the local orphans' court. In 1728, a Jacob Phillip was made Isaac's guardian until he turned twenty and became eligible to inherit his father's vast properties.

The Next Generations and the Fever Years

In 1720, Lewes was home to about sixty families, three hundred people in all. There was a general store downtown, a smithy, several mercantile shops and three very active churches. Dotted around the town were small subsistence and tenant farms, each about one mile apart, growing corn, rye, wheat and tobacco. Every farm had a cow, hogs, chickens and perhaps an ox. The wealthy landholders owned slaves who worked their personal farms of twenty to thirty acres, made clothing and handled domestic chores.

Missing were the Siconese. While visiting Lewes in 1726, the Reverend William Beckett reported, "We have but a few Indians." Of those who remained, Beckett wrote they "seem obstinate to the means of conversion."

The term *namesake*, describing the tradition of naming children for their ancestors, first came into use in the colonies in 1632. As time went on and the Wiltbancks grew in numbers, many of their children were named Isaac, Abraham and Cornelius, creating significant opportunities for this author's and readers' confusion. The following chart may help guide readers through the following generations.

Generation 2: After coming of age at twenty, the first Cornelius's only son, the orphaned Isaac (2), a grandson to Helms and Jane, lived and farmed at the Preserve. His marriage to Mary Rowland resulted in seven children, including two sons who survived: Cornelius (3) (1745–1797) and Samuel (1758–1833). (Another Cornelius [2] had been born forty-five years earlier to Helms' youngest son, Isaac [1], in 1700.)

Generation 3: When Cornelius's son Isaac (2) died a widower at age forty-eight in 1769, he left his large estate to all seven of his children.

HELMANIAS WILTBANCK
1625–1683

The Preserve	Hopewell/Pilottown Rd.	Tower Hill/CLEAR
CORNELIUS	ABRAHAM	ISAAC
1665–1724	*1661–1731*	*1672–1708*
ISAAC (2)	ABRAHAM (2)	CORNELIUS (2)
1721–1769	*1700–1761*	*1700–1741*
	JACOB	
CORNELIUS (3)	*1702–1761*	
1745–1797		
SAMUEL	ABRAHAM (3)	JOHN
1758–1833	*1732–1782*	*1731–1792*
DAVID		CORNELIUS (4)
1789–1863		*1756–1813*
		REV. JAMES
		1764–1842

Chart of descendants from the three sons of Helmanias Wiltbanck. *Ray Daminger.*

Cornelius (3), as the oldest, received double shares and was given authority by the court to distribute the land and, in some cases, purchase it from his siblings. The Preserve was among the properties Cornelius (3) kept for himself. Isaac's (2) two youngest children—Lydia, four, and Samuel, ten—were assigned by the orphans' court as wards of Samuel Rowland, Mary's brother. Eight years later, Lydia chose her oldest brother, Cornelius (3), to be her guardian instead.

Cornelius's younger brother Samuel married and resettled in New Castle County. He later served as a solider in the Revolutionary War and died at seventy-four in his home at White Clay Creek, while Cornelius (3) remained in Lewes.

During the eighteenth century, land ownership in Lewes passed from person to person largely through inheritance, with acreage altered by agreements, court assignments and other exchanges. Few deeds exist from that period to track the Preserve's trail of owners. However, family records show that the original Preserve—still 1,155 feet wide and stretching a mile back to Pagan Creek—continued to be owned, lived on and farmed by direct descendants of Helms and his son Cornelius Wiltbanck (1) over five

consecutive generations. By the third generation, the spelling of the family name had been shortened to Wiltbank.

Generation 4: Cornelius (3), son of Isaac, grandson of Cornelius (1) and guardian of his younger sister Lydia, married Rachel Hazzard in 1770. Like his brother Samuel, and his cousins Abraham and John, Cornelius was a staunch patriot during the Revolutionary War (1775–83). His wife, Rachel, with Lydia and her five sons, maintained a large home garden for beans,

Mid-eighteenth-century Lewes as captured by Stanley Massey Arthurs, a student of N.C. Wyeth. *Courtesy Lewes Historical Society.*

squash, turnips, cabbage and carrots and a coop for chickens. Half an acre behind their house was reserved for hog pens and grazing. Cornelius (3) also maintained the estate named Cain on the land at the Broadkill River where his grandfather and Jane Maud had built their grain mill eighty years earlier.

In the late eighteenth century, epidemics of yellow fever and smallpox began to cause a disastrous number of deaths among Delaware colonists, taking a particular toll on young families. Although Lewes was remote, ships carrying travelers were arriving from New York, New England and Philadelphia, all active sites of urban plague. Some passengers came ashore from schooners laying over in the bay, awaiting better weather to proceed up the river or out to sea.

Through these "fever years," the lives of generations of early Lewes families were shortened, families merged, children were taken in and remarriages were common. The orphans' court in Lewes ensured children received their just inheritance and were not taken advantage of by their guardians.

This was a difficult period for the Wiltbanks, when fever transmitted by unrelenting mosquitoes from the nearby marshland plagued the town. Fresh sea breezes helped relieve the families above the stream along Pilot Road, but early death still stalked the last generation of male Wiltbancks who were descended from Helms and Jane.

Generation 5: Of Cornelius (3) and Rachel's five sons, only David, the youngest (1789–1863), lived to have children of his own, and just one of David's own three sons survived early childhood. How did they deal with such tragedy?

By 1820, more than 80 percent of Lewes residents belonged to local churches where families like the Wiltbanks were promised eternal salvation—depending, however, on whether they had lived righteous lives. The older people became, the more they feared eternal damnation for their sins. But it was also believed that the younger children were when they died, the more likely their souls were to go to heaven. This provided slight comfort to grieving families.

Cornelius's son David represented the fifth and last generation of Wiltbancks to own Helms's beloved *pra serve* over 148 years. David wrote about "living on land that had passed from father to son since it first became a part of Helmanus Wiltbanck's extensive holdings."

THE FORGOTTEN WILTBANKS

It is worth taking a brief detour now from the owners of the Preserve to John Wiltbank, a grandson of Helms's son Isaac (1), whose enormous contributions have faded from public view.

As noted, Helms's youngest son, Isaac, inherited 140 acres south of the Preserve that extended to the Lewes town boundary line. He also acquired another 200 acres at Tower Hill, increasing his estate there to 334 acres. In 1698, Isaac purchased 100 more acres four miles south of town, and later that year, 15 acres within the town of Lewes. Sickly all his life, Isaac (1) died at just thirty-six in 1708. His wife, Elizabeth, inherited "one third of my personal estate Lands, Houses, Household stuff, cattle, negroes, Debts and instruments."

Isaac's son, Cornelius (2), received the balance of his father's properties. He later married Comfort Roads, a descendant of Helms Wiltbancks's mortal enemy, Dr. John Rhoads. Cornelius and Comfort made their home at the 344-acre Tower Hill estate.

Cornelius (2), who died at forty-one, may be best remembered as the father of John Wiltbanck, the most accomplished of all his family, born at Tower Hill in 1731. In 1750, when he was nineteen, John married Mary Stockley, just turned fourteen, an exceptionally beautiful girl. Mary's father, Woodman, an attorney, had moved with his wife in 1710 to Indian River Hundred (now Angola) from Somerset, Maryland, after receiving title to Bradford Hall, a 1,150-acre estate there. John, who intended to become a lawyer himself, brought Mary to Tower Hill, where he farmed and studied law. They had their first child, Comfort, in 1751, then yet another Cornelius (4) in 1756, followed by Elizabeth and James.

A natural and astute leader of men, John rose to positions of authority quickly. He was commissioned in both 1767 and 1773 as a justice of the peace for Sussex County, then elected in 1775 to Delaware's first provisional assembly.

John was known in Lewes as a "Torry sympathizer," or friend of the king, which made his continued advancement noteworthy. However, he had apparently inherited his ancestor Helms's ability to juggle allegiances when necessary.

In Lewes, emotions ran high between Tories and Patriots. John had to personally intervene to save staunch Whig patriot Henry Fischer when an incensed Tory crowd took an axe to the "Liberty pole" in front of his house and carried it around the town, cheering "hurrah" for the king. Thanks to Wiltbank's interference, Fischer "got clear of the mob and safe into my house."

After Delaware and then the Congressional Congress voted for independence from Great Britain in 1776, Caesar Rodney, a contemporary and Lewes native, was able to enlist John's help in preparing for the coming war against Great Britain. Over the next year, John coauthored the first Delaware constitution, through which the three colonies established their own state, free of Pennsylvania's rule.

John and Caesar Rodney had the stature and influence to raise the funds and donations of crops from other wealthy landowners to fund Delaware troops in the Revolutionary War. John's aversion to borrowing, or using overvalued Delaware or Continental currency, resulted in Delaware having the lowest debt of any of the thirteen colonies at the end of the war.

IN 1777, JOHN WILTBANK was commissioned major of the Sussex County Military Regiment and military treasurer for Sussex County. In that critical role, John Wiltbank managed and disbursed the resources to support Delaware's troops, in particular its First Regiment of 320 men who were dispatched (and reinforced) for four years—the longest service of any colony—to fight in battles from New York to South Carolina. Many of those men, captained by Colonel David Hall, were from Lewes.

As the war proceeded, John was elected to Delaware's first legislature counsel (today's state senate), receiving the most votes (524) of any candidate, and then named chief justice of the Sussex County Court of Common Pleas. Throughout this turbulent time, John continued in the critical role of military treasurer. He acquired a second estate, Dover, where he and Mary lived while he carried out his many governing responsibilities nearby. One of the nation's first Fourth of July celebrations took place in Lewes in 1777. After the war ended in 1783, John Wiltbank resumed his career there as a respected judge.

When their son Cornelius (4) married and brought his bride to Tower Hill, John and Mary made their primary residence at the 140-acre estate, named Clear, adjacent to town and below the Preserve. Their home, built in the 1740s, sat on the boundary line of Lewes and is today open to visitors as the Hiram-Burton House, a principal attraction of the Lewes Historical Society.

Believers in the importance of education, John and Mary donated a lot at Shipcarpenter

Portrait of the Honorable John Wiltbank. *Lewes History Museum.*

Hiram Rodney Burton House (*on right*), campus of Lewes Historical Society, former home of John and the Reverend James Wiltbanck *Deny Howeth.*

and Second Streets for Lewes's first school not affiliated with a church. The land was deeded to fourteen "leading citizens of the town," including Ryves Holt, Henry Fisher, Samuel Rowland and David Hall. Known as the Little Schoolhouse, the school provided basic education to the children of Lewes, including four future governors, for the next one hundred years. John and Mary remained active with the school for the rest of their lives.

John passed away at their Dover estate in 1792 at age sixty-one; Mary died three years later. In his will, John assigned ownership of his slaves to their children with the provision that each slave be freed when they reached the age of thirty-four and a half. He left Tower Hill to his son Cornelius (4), who enjoyed life as a "gentleman" philanthropist and served as a warden at St. Peter's Church, where his brother, James, had become pastor after graduating from Princeton University.

The Lewes estate went to James, who lived at the Shipcarpenter Street house, where he and his wife took in boarders while he served both as a pastor and principal of the Lewes Academy. The couple left for Philadelphia in 1809 when James became chaplain of the U.S. Navy. In 1813, the Reverend James Wiltbank conveyed the front 27.5 acres of the estate, including the family's house, to Captain Thomas Rodney. James Wiltbank was later named provost of the University of Pennsylvania. He is buried in Philadelphia.

John Wiltbank family cemetery on New Road, 1985. *Lewes Historical Society.*

John Wiltbank family cemetery, 2024. *Deny Howeth.*

John and Mary were interred in the Wiltbank family cemetery at Hopewell, across from Tower Hill, where nine other of their descendants would later be buried. Those included Cornelius (4) and his wife, Ann; their son John and daughter, Comfort, who was interred with an infant; Cornelius's second wife, Esther; and their grandson, John. A photograph from 1985 shows their burial site in good repair. However, just forty years later, the small fifty-by-fifty-foot cemetery sits abandoned, hidden in a thorny patch of briars and junk trees just off New Road.

As of this writing, the GLF and Lewes Historical Society are exploring ways to restore and maintain the cemetery as a more fitting memorial for this branch of the Wiltbank family who contributed so much to Lewes, Sussex County and Delaware.

Chapter 2

THE WEST FAMILY AND OTHER OWNERS

THE NINETEENTH CENTURY WITH THE WESTS AND THE MUSTARDS

A survey from 1807 shows only eighty buildings of all types in Lewes. Over the next fifty years, no significant population growth occurred in the small town. Apart from a few oyster-shell lanes, the roads remained dirt through the early twentieth century.

While a number of attractive houses had been built along Pilot Road, on Second Street and Shipcarpenter Street, many of the original colonial houses were still in use. Some had been expanded, while others still consisted of one large room with a fireplace, a loft and a hard-packed dirt floor. One such house remained occupied on Chestnut Street as late as 2014.

Robert West was the namesake grandson of the original West, a contemporary of Helms's children, who had arrived from Great Britain in 1717 and died in Lewes in 1742. The first Robert West married Elizabeth Lewis, whose father, Peter, had consorted with Captain William Kidd during his ten-day layover in Lewes harbor in 1699.

Peter Lewis, William Orr and George Thompson—rumored to have been "old pirates" themselves—did business with Kidd and spent the night on his *Adventure Galley*. They got into trouble the next day trying to smuggle calico cloth, muslin, silk and sugar to sell past the port collector and were rebuked by none other than William Penn.

By 1818, David Wiltbank had sold the Preserve to Robert West. That year, the Lewes commissioners were rushing to incorporate and expand the

Early nineteenth-century Second Street home, still in place. *Lewes Historical Society.*

Early small Colonial home, restored. *Lewes Historical Society.*

town's boundaries, to forestall an attempt by Sussex County to claim all the land surrounding Lewes, including Cape Henlopen and the Great Marsh. Robert West was noted as owning the Preserve in the Lewes Town Act of 1818, which defined new boundaries as follows: "The said town of Lewes shall begin at the north corner of Robert West's land where it intersects the line of William Russell's land on the road leading to Pilot town."

West (2) married Naomi Thompson, who brought with her substantial landholdings. They had seven children, all boys. Though only four sons survived to adulthood, by 1818, Lewes was home to numerous Wests.

The Wests' oldest son, Lewis, was the same age as David Wiltbanck, the final family owner of the Preserve, who was by then establishing his new home at Cornelius's (3) Broadkill plantation, Cain. When Lewis married his wife, Elizabeth Howard, she owned considerable land in and around Lewes. Thus, over ninety-five years, the Wests existed as a prominent local family, though unlike most old Lewes families, none remained in Lewes in later years.

African Americans in Lewes

While there were as many White indentured servants as slaves in the Delaware's early eighteenth century, the number of African Americans, both free and enslaved, had been growing steadily throughout the new state, as the chart below illustrates, then declined rapidly after the mid-1800s.

African Americans in Delaware

Year	Free	Enslaved
1790	3,899	8,887
1800	8,268	6,153
1810	13,136	6,153
1820–30	N/A	N/A
1840	16,919	2,605
1860	19,829	1,798

Several factors influenced this trend. First, soil exhaustion caused a decline in tobacco growing and hence the need for slave labor. Religious influence also caused many landowners to reject the buying, selling and holding of slaves. Lastly, improved and early mechanized farm equipment began to replace manual labor.

The AME cemetery on Pilottown Road, where some 550 souls are interred. *Deny Howeth.*

By mid-century, the inhuman practice of slavery was drawing to a close in Lewes and Sussex County. One of the last slaveholders, Sheppard P. Houston, lived in Lewes. One night, during a heavy storm, three of his four slaves escaped. They were joined at Lewes Beach by Isaac White, twenty-two, who was fleeing from the Lewes blacksmith, a Wiltbank. The four young men climbed into a small skiff and rowed through the storm across the Delaware Bay to New Jersey, which was not a slave state. From there, William Cope, John and Henry Boice and Isaac White secured passage on an oyster boat to Philadelphia and freedom.

Some 238 Blacks (23 percent of the local population) lived in Lewes in 1830, including both slaves and others who had been freed. Six Black families lived along the Preserve's canal bank in 1833. Two of those were a former West family slave, Peter "Cato" Lewis and his adult son, also named Peter—perhaps, whimsically, after the Wests' piratical ancestor.

On his father's passing in 1833, Lewis West inherited the Preserve, where he and Elizabeth had been living and farming. One of his first acts was to convey two acres of land at the far right corner of the Preserve to Cato Lewis. The land was to be used for Cato's house and as a Black cemetery.

A year earlier, Cato and Peter had also purchased, via sheriff's sale, half an acre of the Preserve's bank land on the canal for use as perhaps the first Black-owned boatbuilding operation in the country. Eliza Ann Maull Marshall, who lived at 356 Pilot Road, contributed a corncrib there as a place to hold services, and Richard Allen of Philadelphia, founder of the

African Methodist Episcopal (AME) Church, stopped regularly to preach during his salt-harvesting trips along the canal. In time, the corncrib was moved across the street behind the cemetery, where it served as the first St. George's AME Church, with Peter Lewis as its preacher.

In 1918 and 1920, two local workingmen would die and be buried in the AME cemetery: George L. Wait Wiltbank (1846–1918) and Caesar Wiltbank (1838–1920), both of whom had been born into slavery.

LEWIS AND ELIZABETH WEST had two children: a daughter, Mary, and a son, Robert West (3). Like most of their relatives, they belonged to the tall Presbyterian church recently built on Kings Highway in 1832 for the recently arrived Reverend Cornelius Mustard.

After happily finding Mary in his congregation, the Reverend Cornelius married Lewis West's pretty daughter in 1834. Their first child, David Mustard, was born later that same year, and a second son, Robert West Mustard, so named for Mary's brother, came along in 1839.

Sadly, Mary West Mustard died in 1842 at just twenty-eight, after which Robert West Mustard, three, and his older brother, David Lewis (D.L.), eight, were raised by a single father who was in great demand, preaching at Lewes, Rehoboth and Cool Springs and teaching at the church school.

Robert and Clementine West. *Lewes Historical Society.*

The Reverend Mustard's Presbyterian church on Kings Highway. *Lewes Historical Society.*

Mary's brother, Robert West, continued to live in their family home at the Preserve until, at age twenty-eight, he married Clementine Faust and built a second house next door. In honor of Mary and her husband, Robert and Clementine named their first child Margaret Cornelius (Maggie) when she was born in 1841. It would be seventeen years before they had two more daughters, Clara in 1858 and Louse in 1861, the latter of whom died at birth.

West's neighbor William Russell made his fortune tanning hides. The hides were boiled in twenty vats farther north on Pilot Road, on bank land across from homes he owned, then treated with crushed sap from white oaks. The odor was unbearable. Russell then dried and shipped the hides to Philadelphia and used his ships to bring back limestone, which he sold locally. In 1840,

DOWN PILOTTOWN ROAD

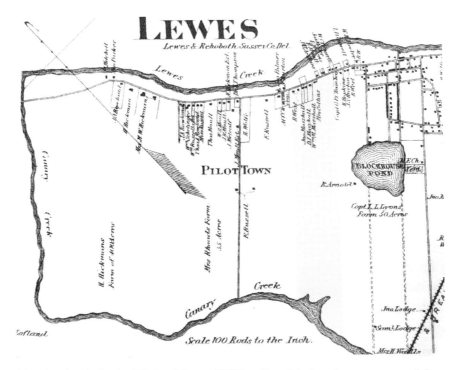

Map showing the lands of Robert West and William Russell before sixty-seven acres of the Preserve were sold to Russell. *D.G. Beers, Map of Lewes and Rehoboth,* Atlas of the State of Delaware, *1868, p. 89.*

Russell laid the first section of New Road over the old dirt Russell Lane, to improve access to his extensive inland holdings that stretched back to the Great Marsh. In years to come, Russell would acquire the sixty-seven back acres of the Preserve leading to Canary Creek, though the exact date is unknown. A map from 1868 still shows West as the Preserve's owner.

ROBERT WEST OWNED AND operated a profitable ship chandler's store, which had been founded in Lewes by his father. When Lewis West died at age sixty-eight in 1857, Robert, forty-five, also inherited the Preserve. That same year, Robert hired his nephew, Robert West Mustard, the son of his deceased sister Mary, as a clerk and partner in his firm. The two men reportedly became very close.

Robert West Mustard (*standing*) with two unidentified men. *Lewes Historical Society.*

By 1861, West's young clerk, R.W. Mustard, was growing nervous over the Civil War and pending Union army draft, both of which he intended to avoid. Within the year, with help from his brother David and uncle Robert, R.W. Mustard joined a group of young men fleeing by ship to Europe.

FROM LEWES TO SHANGHAI

The use of pilots to help large ships safely navigate the Delaware River dates to as early as 1650, when Siconese Indians are known to have played that role. The first river pilot was officially licensed by the Crown in 1694. It wasn't until 1756 that the first complete chart of the Delaware River and Bay was drawn by Joshua Fisher of Lewes. By then, twenty-two river pilots in Lewes had been licensed to guide ships arriving at the bay upriver.

While Lewes was still a remote outpost, its status as a seaport gave it more contact with the outside world than other inland communities. Whereas 90 percent of the people from Sussex County were farmers, the wealthiest Lewes residents included river pilots, merchants and shipbuilders. Most residents, of course, still farmed, many as tenants. While poor, they were at least self-sufficient. Some sold fish, oysters, timber, cedar shingles, flour, corn and wheat for export. In 1851, a Western Union telegraph office opened to support import and export shipping activities.

In 1859, a cousin of Robert West's, William Arthur West, twenty-six, was working as a third-generation river pilot. He had recently completed

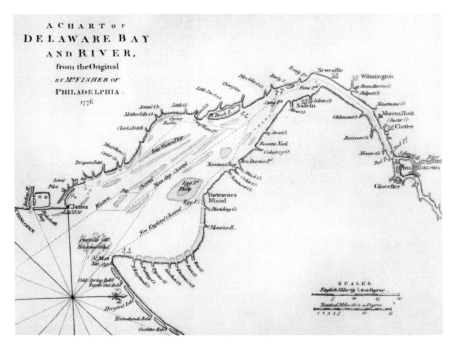

Original 1776 chart of the Delaware Bay by Joshua Fisher. *From* Gentlemen's Magazine, *1779.*

five years of arduous training under his father, Bailey Art, which included forty-eight trips up the Delaware to Philadelphia and back. William was navigating the windjammer *Sultan* downriver from Philadelphia. They had just approached the Delaware Bay when a massive storm forced the ship far out into the Atlantic.

The *Sultan* was on its way from Philadelphia to Shanghai, loaded down with coal. Once en route, Captain Berry would not turn back. And so William West found himself on a four-month voyage to China, from the South Atlantic through the Indian Ocean to the China Sea. He had one other passenger to keep him company: Berry's wife, Sarah.

Sarah was not an enthusiastic traveler. In her Bible, she wrote, "I shall feel relieved if we get there in safety, God grant we may. None die too soon who live for heaven!" Sarah appears to have taken it upon herself to instruct the rough young river pilot. Upon their safe arrival, she gave William her personal Bible with the following inscription:

> *October 5th, 1859*
> *William A. West*
> *From your friend S.B. Berry*
> *Read the scriptures*
> *Shanghai, China*

In 1859, few Americans lived and worked in Shanghai, though more would arrive soon. In short order, William West found employment with a British trading firm, Augustine Heard & Co. First, he was given command of a heavily armed clipper ship, the *Wanderer*, which he sailed along the coast from Hong Kong to Peking, avoiding pirates while his employers plied the illegal opium trade. In 1861, after West had proven himself, Heard assigned him as captain of a freighter. In time, by then with another firm, West was captaining a large steamship, the *Kiang-loon*, ferrying up to five hundred passengers at a time down the one-hundred-mile Yangtze River.

After a spell in Europe, Robert West Mustard traveled to Shanghai to look up his second cousin. William put Mustard to work as a purser on his riverboat.

R.W. MUSTARD WAS DETERMINED to make his fortune in China's thriving import/export business, earning commissions from deals he could broker between Chinese and U.S. companies. He left William's employ after several

A schooner like Captain Berry's as it may have appeared, swept by a storm into the Atlantic Ocean. *Adobe Stock.*

years to start his own small company, which was dwarfed by much larger British firms that had their own ships and warehouses and offered many more services.

In 1866, his former employer in Lewes, Robert West, departed the Preserve and his ship chandler's store in Lewes for a trip to Shanghai. It can be assumed his trip had at least two purposes: first, to see for himself, and for the Reverend Mustard, how his namesake, R.W. Mustard, was faring and second, to discuss with William West the prospect of marriage to Robert's daughter Maggie. Having failed to sire a son, Robert appears to have been shopping for a worthy heir.

In an era when girls married as early as fourteen, Maggie was twenty-eight, still single and living with her parents at the Preserve. Maggie was known in Lewes for her "wit, intellect, strength of character and sense of humor." In other words, she was outspoken and strong-willed—characteristics that may have appealed to the rugged river pilot, who was also making long-term plans for his eventual return home. While Robert was visiting in China, the sale of a lot at the front of the Preserve was handled on his behalf by David L. Mustard.

Maggie West and William West. *Lewes Historical Society.*

R.W. Mustard and William West returned together to Lewes in 1869, four years after the Civil War ended. West visited his parents and, likely by prior arrangement, briefly courted and married his second cousin, Maggie, Robert West's oldest child.

R.W. Mustard's reason for returning to Lewes was to liquidate $3,000 in assets, which, combined with a loan from William West, helped replenish his business accounts. He promised his father he would use the money wisely. Once back in China, however, R.W. started an ill-fated effort to process, can and sell dried, condensed (and inedible) eggs, modeled after the Borden Milk Company's more successful new condensed milk product.

IN THE YEARS FOLLOWING, due to the arrival of the Junction & Breakwater railroad in 1870, Lewes and the Preserve began to change dramatically. Regular train service opened the small town to new opportunities for trade, travel, local industries, tourism and communication. The first rail station, built at Kings Highway, was soon surrounded by canneries, a train repair station, a granary mill, a forge and other businesses.

Many new Victorian-style homes (150 within seventeen years) and commercial buildings began to be built, and Lewes's population soon nearly doubled to 1,800. The new "mansions" in town were two or three stories tall with wraparound porches, imported Victorian accents and central heating.

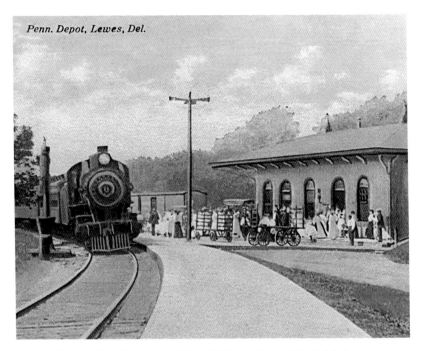

Penn. Depot, Lewes, Del.

The first Lewes railroad station on King's Highway. *Lewes Historical Society.*

The late nineteenth-century Rabbit's Ferry Home, now on the LHS campus. *Lewes Historical Society.*

Pilot Town, Lewes, Del.

Pilots resided in most of the homes along Pilottown Road. *Lewes Historical Society.*

The core of the town's social and business activities was along Second Street, but some of the largest homes were built on Pilot Road by legendary river pilots—Chambers, Kelly, Virden, Marshall and Bertran.

In Lewes, R.W. Mustard's brother, David Lewis Mustard, had become a Penn-educated physician. Instead of practicing, in 1871, he opened a pharmacy in Lewes called Mustard & Co. Two years later, his brother-in-law, Ebe Tunnell, joined him as a drug clerk. Over time, their drugstore expanded to include hardware and numerous "sundries," the equivalent of a department store. They bottled and sold their own Mustard & Co. remedies: one to keep flies off horses, another a salve for sore feet—and, of course, cough medicine. Mustard & Co. also carried items imported from Robert's firm in China. Their store became known for displaying "curiosities" in its front window, such as a rare Indian cornmill, an abnormally large hen's egg and twin cucumbers.

WITHIN A YEAR OF his return home in 1869, and just months after his marriage, William West was on his way back to Shanghai. Maggie, though, was not going to be left behind as a spinster wife. In 1870, she boarded the new transcontinental train to California and, from there, followed William on the Pacific steamship *Great Republic* to Yokohama, then on to Shanghai.

Second Street stores in the early twentieth century. *Lewes Historical Society.*

Maggie spent her first weeks in China living with William on board the *Kiang-loong* until he bought them a house. A year later, Maggie gave birth to a daughter, Mary Clementine, who sadly died after just 265 days. When she became pregnant again, Maggie refused to risk the life of another infant to Shanghai's unhealthy climate and unsanitary hospital conditions. Instead, she booked passage on a sailing ship, which took her home via a slow, rough passage around Cape Horn.

After many weeks at sea, a very pregnant Maggie arrived in Camden, New Jersey. From there, she crossed the Delaware River via ferry to Philadelphia where her second daughter, Margaret Theodora, was soon born in an American hospital on October 7, 1874. Also in 1874, Robert and Clementine West's daughter, Clara, came home to Lewes from studying in Philadelphia to marry a young man named—Robert Mustard.

Maggie and her infant daughter, Margaret, returned to China in 1875, where she and William socialized with R.W. Mustard and attended balls for the U.S. centennial celebration in Kim-kiang and Shanghai. Later that year, the William West family, plus R.W. Mustard, steamed back again to Lewes.

This time, William and Maggie returned home permanently, perhaps due to her father's failing health. R.W. came back to collect his share of the inheritance from his father, who had recently died. Ironically, the Reverend Mustard had never approved of Robert's infatuation with earning money.

Now, his lifelong savings would help pay for R.W. Mustard's last chapter as an entrepreneur.

Always frail and a confirmed bachelor, R.W. Mustard had become ill from the unhealthy Shanghai climate. He stayed one year with his brother David in Lewes to recuperate and reconnect with his uncle Robert West, his former employer and namesake. During the year he was home, R.W. also formed a close relationship with his nephew, Lewis West Mustard, and Lewis's wife. After regaining his health, R.W. Mustard returned to Shanghai in 1877 to continue pursuing his elusive fortune.

Robert West passed away at his home in Lewes in 1878. In his will, he left the Preserve to Clementine and made mention of it having

Robert West Mustard, after securing his fortune. *Lewes Historical Society.*

been reduced over time to "33 acres, part of what Robert inherited from his father Lewis West." Meanwhile, Maggie and William West had taken up residence in the Germantown section of Philadelphia. It was a difficult year, for after Maggie's father's passing, they suffered the death of yet another child, a son, Robert Bailey, at only six months of age, also in 1878.

Clementine continued to live at the Preserve, where William, Maggie and her granddaughter visited often. Clementine died there in 1887, after which the Preserve was inherited by William West and its two houses were apparently rented out. A map of 1890–1900 Lewes shows both West homes occupied by members of the Marshall and Maull families.

In 1891, David Mustard and Ebe Tunnell cofounded a Lewes newspaper, the *Delaware Pilot*. In 1897, Ebe Tunnell was elected governor of Delaware after an unsuccessful campaign five years earlier. Over the years, David did not hesitate to editorialize his own dictums in the *Delaware Pilot*. In 1898, the Wilmington *Evening Journal* took him to task for "persistently antagonizing the running of Sunday trains to Rehoboth." In its own editorial, the *Journal* characterized Mustard as one who "construes 'Remember the Sabbath and keep it holy' as 'Remember the Sabbath and make it miserable.'"

BACK IN SHANGHAI, ROBERT West Mustard at last struck gold when he secured exclusive rights from the American Tobacco Company to distribute cigarettes in China. By 1898, twenty million cigarettes were passing through the Mustard & Co. warehouses every month—in addition to tomatoes imported from Lewes!

R.W. finally had the life he'd sought, including a mansion with eleven servants and horses at the Shanghai Race Club. Heavily involved with Shanghai's social scene, Robert politely dismissed his family's urging to return to Lewes for his health when his nephew visited him in 1899.

Robert West Mustard died in 1900, three months after his brother David had passed away at his Lewes home at 236 Second Street. After serving as governor, Ebe Tunnell, a bachelor, returned to live with his widowed sister, David's wife, in Lewes. He continued as an owner of the *Delaware Pilot* and was named president of Farmer's Bank.

R.W. left his thriving import business to his nephew, Lewis West Mustard, who traveled with his wife and children to China several times, then sold his interest to Robert's former partner. For years thereafter, Lewis West Mustard and his wife headlined the social scene in Lewes; their New Year's Eve party was the event of the year. Lewis also purchased the first automobile in Lewes, bringing employment to a host of youth who were charged with watering down the dirt streets to diminish the dust thrown up by his tires.

The adventurous Captain William West died in Philadelphia in 1904, and Maggie passed away there in 1910. Prior to then, in 1905, the Preserve had been purchased from William's estate by another local river pilot, William Cottingham.

RAILROADS AND RIVER PILOTS

Earlier, in 1898, an extension of the railroad lines in Lewes had made a major impact on the Preserve. It began when the Queen Anne Railroad secured permission to construct a rail line from that Maryland county to Lewes Beach and its recently built (but ill-conceived) 1,200-foot iron pier.

Two new spurs were laid. The first entered the Preserve from New Road, then curved up to a new passenger terminal on Pilottown Road at Queen Anne Lane. From there, the spur crossed the Lewes canal on a wooden bridge to the beach, then circled back to the original Lewes station.

The second track from Maryland split off at New Road and ran below the Preserve, across Savannah Road to the Kings Highway station. There, passengers could connect with the existing Maryland-Delaware-Virginia (or MDV) line to Rehoboth Beach.

Bird's Eye View, Lewes, Del.

This is one of the prettiest little town I have been in for some time.

A locomotive steaming across the flats from Queen Anne station to the iron pier. *Lewes Historical Society.*

Trees on the Preserve behind homes along Pilottown Road. *Deny Howeth.*

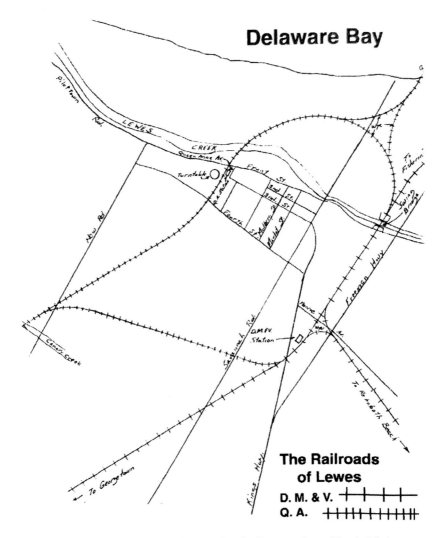

A drawing of the new Queen Anne line crossing the Preserve. *Lewes Historical Society.*

The Queen Anne passenger trains ran on tracks of heavy-gauge steel and wood atop sloped gravel rights-of-way. Ditches were dug alongside the tracks to manage draining. This ended farming on the front half, or about 50 percent of the Preserve. A forest of trees began to grow behind the homes on Pilot Road.

BY THE EARLY TWENTIETH century, ninety-one river pilots lived in Lewes, up from thirty just years before. Eight trim schooners were shared by groups of

The first pilot ship *Philadelphia*. *Lewes Historical Society.*

five to six pilots and docked at the inlet farther up Pilot Road, from where the pilots could tack quickly across the bay to intercept incoming ships. One schooner was named the *Ebe Tunnell.*

The first man to scale the side of a ship on its Jacob's ladder and set foot on deck got the piloting job. The competition became so costly, intense and occasionally bloody that a pilots' association was formed in 1896 to manage assignments, own the pilot boats, set rates and pool and distribute income.

By 1900, the association had commissioned a specially designed steel steamer, the 148-foot *Philadelphia*, to be anchored at the mouth of the Delaware Bay, where it could stop larger ships as they entered and send pilots to them in small wooden skiffs. Several pilots were assigned to await service on the steamer's open deck.

When William Cottingham purchased the Preserve from the West estate in 1905, the houses built along Pilot Road were nearly all owned by river pilots. Five of those now sat in front of the Preserve. The splendor of their homes set pilots apart as the elite class of Lewes and located them close to

Train crossing Pilottown Road onto the Preserve at Queen Anne station. *Lewes Historical Society.*

the inlet and to the pilot boat that could call for their services at any hour. Pilots could begin work as apprentices at twenty-one and became eligible for a rich retirement after twenty years of service (though some could, and did, serve until forced to retire at seventy). Over the decades, pilots and their descendants became the majority of Lewes's community leaders—and among the wealthiest. Opportunities for piloting work were closely handed down from father to son.

HEAVY COSTS FORCED THE Queen Anne Railroad out of operation in 1904, after which the tracks across the Preserve were acquired by the Pennsylvania Railroad to haul freight to and from ships in Lewes Bay to northern and western markets. Thus, during his ownership of the Preserve, from 1905 on, pilot Will Cottingham experienced countless trains sounding loud warnings as they crossed Pilot Road a few houses down and then chugged behind his property, spewing heavy clouds of steam, dust and cinders from the wood they burned. The MDV line was not popular with locals, who alternately called it the "mad, dirty and viscous" and the "many dirty visits" railroad.

The twenty years of train activity across the Preserve came to an end in 1918 when the wooden rail bridge at Queen Anne Avenue was removed to enable the widening and dredging of the Lewes-Rehoboth Canal. Today, the raised mounds of land that carried tracks across the front of the Preserve still exist, as do the ditches alongside them. Pieces of coal and cinders can still be found there.

EDGAR AND THOMAS INGRAM, ENTREPRENEURS

After fourteen years, in 1919, Will Cottingham sold the Preserve to two local businessmen, Edgar and Thomas Ingram. Only one lot along the Preserve, adjacent to the AME cemetery, remained unsold and still part of the Preserve. Since 1856, ownership of that parcel had been contested by St. Peter's Church, which claimed the Rowland family had given it to the vestry in 1716 as a site for its first church, which was built instead on Second Street.

Brothers Edgar and Thomas Ingram were important Lewes business and civic leaders during the boom years following the arrival of the railroad. The Ingrams are one of Lewes's oldest families, dating back to Abraham Ingram in 1720. They, too, produced generations of descendants, and unlike the Wests, Ingrams remain in Lewes today.

Edgar (1869–1956) had served as the agent at the Queen Anne station on Pilot Road in 1898. By 1919, at age fifty, the short, bald, bespectacled entrepreneur owned a bustling hardware store on Second Street; later, he sold that and purchased a prosperous insurance agency.

Since his house on Pilot Road sat next to the Queen Anne station, Edgar knew Will Cottingham and of his interest in selling the Preserve. Edgar also knew the pending removal of the spur line would increase the land's value and that he could sell the remaining lot as well.

Edgar's brother and partner Thomas (1874–1944), forty-five at the time, was a director of the Lewes and Rehoboth Building Society and the first president of Sussex Trust, whose new building on Second Street with its clock and stone façade opened in 1911 and remains a bank today. Thomas was well positioned to help finance their investment.

Edgar bought out Thomas's interest a year later. He then sold the Preserve and the remaining undeveloped lot next to the AME cemetery to Captain John Steele Wingate in 1922. By that year, the population of Lewes had reached 2,200.

CAPTAIN JOHN STEELE WINGATE

The shifting shoals around Cape Henlopen at the entrance to Delaware Bay had always been treacherous to ships. By 1800, more than two hundred shipwrecks had been recorded there, and many hundreds of unknown sailors were buried in a mass grave beneath today's Delaware River and Bay Ferry parking lot and visitor center, now known as the most haunted site in Lewes. Construction of the Cape Henlopen Lighthouse in 1767 and directional lights on the new breakwaters (1828–51) reduced the carnage, but the need for lifeguard stations remained acute.

A Lewes native, John Wingate was a lifelong coast guard captain and the last of the old sailing vessel era. He first enlisted at the Lewes station in 1909, after which he took command as keeper of the stations (spaced three miles apart) at Rehoboth Beach, then the Cape.

A Lewes breakwater and light, constructed to be a safe haven for sailing ships. *Lewes Historical Society.*

Lewes lifeguard station. *Lewes Historical Society.*

Wingate and his six-man crews launched in open boats in the worst conditions possible to rescue crew and passengers from ships that had run aground in the treacherous waters. If their boats could not launch, rescuers used a Lyle gun to shoot a lifeline to the ship, over which a "lifecare capsule" could be sent to carry passengers to shore. Being jammed together into the eleven-foot metal casket with open portholes and then dragged over and under thundering surf was so traumatizing to already terrified passengers that use of the capsule was discontinued after a few years.

Wingate was on duty when the Cape Henlopen Lighthouse fell in 1926. It had been built one mile inland, but the "moving dunes" of Lewes caused its demise after just 159 years. In his memoir, Robert Orr recalls, as a child, looking at the lighthouse from town as he often did, then looking again— "and it was gone."

In 1929, Wingate returned to the Lewes station, where he retired in 1932, during the heart of the Great Depression. He made his home at the same site on the Preserve where the Wiltbank-West-Cottingham houses

Cape Henlopen Lighthouse before its fall. *Lewes Historical Society.*

had stood. After the rail tracks were removed, Wingate left the front right quadrant of the Preserve wooded and continued farming the back. There, centuries of plowing had lowered the land's height by several feet. (This can be seen today by contrasting the height of local cemeteries with the land around them.)

Wingate leased the front section of the Preserve behind his and others' homes along Pilot Road as a grazing pasture for horses owned by local residents Bailey Maull, Ed Jones and Charles Lowe. As noted by Wingate's next-door neighbor Helene Potter, irritated neighbors needed to build fences to keep the horses out of their gardens.

The only access to the Preserve for farm vehicles was via a longtime easement at 360 Pilottown Road, still evident today. Wingate had constructed a cistern and then laid a terra-cotta pipe belowground at the easement to drain storm water from the pasture down the drive and across Pilottown Road into the canal. It remains functioning 120 years later.

Income from his retirement and farming on the Preserve's back acres helped sustain Captain Wingate through post–World War I, the Great Depression and the early days of World War II. In 1940, Wingate sold the last unbuilt lot, next to the AME cemetery, to Franklin Maull, whose friends in

The Preserve in 1937, nineteen years after rail service ended. Farming has resumed on upper left quadrant; trees are growing along the former railroad line. *University of Delaware.*

the vestry of St. Peter's Church signed a release to the lot in 1941. Soon after, Maull resold the lot to William Egan, a president of the Pilot's Association. Egan then built a large house there for his wife and twin daughters, under the proviso that no basement be dug in case there were ancient Rowland graves on the land.

Opposite, top: A proud Lewes man with his horse. *Lewes Historical Society.*

Opposite, bottom: The only entrance to the Preserve. The homes to the left and right are on the original site of the Wiltbanck and West houses. *Deny Howeth.*

Above: Aerial view of the Preserve circa 1956, from a menhaden fish spotter plane. *Lewes Historical Society.*

A local teen named Hazel babysat the twins whenever Egan returned from his three weeks of pilot duty, and a local boy, Bobby Hastings, cared for Egan's lawn and cleared leaf and branch debris from the trees on the Preserve behind their house. (We will hear more about both Hazel and Bobby shortly.)

At that time, the Preserve was about to end its long history as farmland, though other farms still surrounded it as far as the eye could see. Captain Wingate sold the Preserve to a local investor in 1944. He died six years later in 1950 and was buried at the Lewes Presbyterian Church.

The Egan house was acquired in 1960 by William Ingram, a river pilot and the grandson of Thomas Ingram. For decades, Bill Ingram faithfully cut and maintained the grass at the AME cemetery next to his house. His second wife, Doris, remains a cherished Lewes artist.

Chapter 3

THE ROLLINS FAMILY

ISABEL JACOB HAS COMPANY

In 1944, Isabel Jacob assumed responsibility for the Preserve. She was the only woman in a local investment group that held interests in various Lewes properties as well as a local furniture store. Isabel's properties also included the Wingate house and its access road to her new land, a commercial site in town and a bayfront house on Lewes Beach where she chose to live, no doubt to avoid the odors from the fish-processing plant at the end of Pilottown Road.

Isabel discontinued farming on the back acres of the Preserve and allowed trees to grow there again. Soon after her purchase, she sold six one-hundred-foot parcels of the Preserve to other homeowners along Pilottown Road, at the back of their homes, to extend their properties for gardens and recover some of her acquisition costs. This, plus the prior sale of the Egan lot, reduced the Preserve to its current thirty acres, leaving the original historic 1,155-foot frontage behind the nine houses along Pilottown Road unchanged.

In 1945, Isabel added four very active new people to her life. Her daughter, Kitty, had married John Rollins, an engaging, high-energy factory manager from Georgia. After several years of fifteen-hour days overseeing war production for large corporations, John Rollins moved with Kitty and their two young children to Lewes for a respite. They lived at

Bryan Rollins Motors of Lewes, the start of Rollins Inc. *Michelle Rollins.*

first with Isabel at her house behind the dunes on Lewes Beach while John commuted weekly to Towson, Maryland, for work at Bendix. The long drive and workers' resistance to his proposed plant improvements soon became tiresome, and John resigned.

John Rollins was hardworking, ambitious and opportunistic. The Lewes locals weren't sure what to make of the "poor man from Georgia" who had to live with his mother-in-law. John soon showed them. He had been ruminating over the need for a local repair shop for his Ford. John leased Isabel's commercial property in Lewes, obtained a $10,000 loan from Sussex Trust and opened a Ford dealership with his fishing buddy Dory Bryan, a Lewes councilman.

There was a built-in market for the Bryan Rollins dealership in Lewes. The town's two busy fish-processing plants employed 2,000 people, swelling Lewes's population to 3,000. And there were still a significant number of people working at Fort Miles, the army installation built at Cape Henlopen to ward off German naval attacks during World War II.

Most of the fish factory employees were hardworking, well paid African Americans who settled with their families in town. By 1950, 40 percent of Lewes's population was attributable to employment at its two large (and smelly) fish plants, one at the end of Pilottown Road and the other near the entrance to Fort Miles.

THE ROLLINS BROTHERS

A forward-thinking entrepreneur, John soon encouraged his brother, Wayne, to join him in Lewes and invest in his plan to grow Ford dealerships across Delmarva. The brothers were extremely close, having grown up in a three-room house in the rough hills of Georgia with a tiny fireplace, a woodstove and no electricity or plumbing. It was an existence not far removed from colonial days at the Preserve.

Wayne had been pursuing his interest in radio, which had fascinated him since his youth. He bought his first station in Radford, Virginia, learned the business and then joined John in Lewes. Theirs was a good partnership, with John the freewheeling, risk-taking optimist and Wayne the conservative watchdog and manager. Their success was fueled by guts, luck and a good eye for opportunity, lubricated by their charming southern accents and folksy personalities.

The brothers soon added a key third member to their team, Henry Tippie, an accountant from Iowa. Henry was interviewed by the Rollinses over breakfast in Rehoboth Beach. ("If he could find his way here, let's hire him," John said.) The diligent Tippie, his attention focused on Rollins's business documents, ordered his breakfast without looking up. "I won't wait on that rude man again," the waitress said. A few years later, they were married.

In 1949, the Rollins brothers scraped together $12,500, secured another loan and formed Rollins Broadcasting, which Wayne would manage. They then opened WJLW, the first AM radio station in Sussex County. One popular feature was the noon poultry auction broadcast from Selbyville, where buyers from across the United States bid on Delaware chicken flocks. Saturdays featured Ralph Hoebee, "Troubadour of the Eastern Shore," a housepainter from Milton. When local families experienced emergencies, the station put out calls for help.

Within a decade, the Rollins Inc. companies included a regional network of dealerships, ten groundbreaking radio stations (five built around newly popular African American talent), the emerging truck and auto leasing business, billboards in the early '60s and, by 1964, control of the Orkin Pest Control Company in Atlanta, Georgia.

No one could have guessed the small Rollins Inc. venture started in Lewes would one day become a global $50 billion corporation. But all that was still in the future. Then, in postwar Lewes, it was John and Wayne and one of Wayne's two sons, nineteen-year-old Randall Rollins.

RANDY AND PEGGY

High school photos of Randall Rollins and Peggy Hastings. *Amy Kreisler.*

Richard Randall Rollins ("Triple R," as he was called later in life) was strong-willed from the get-go. "He's no trouble at all," his grandmother Claudia said of the baby boy, "as long as you don't contrary him."

Randall led a rowdy teen life in Catoosa Springs, Georgia, little interested in school and often at odds with his father, Wayne. However, the family traits of practicality, honesty and hard work were deeply ingrained in Randall by his parents and both sets of grandparents.

After graduating high school, Randall moved to Lewes to work at his uncle John's dealership, where he put undercoating on cars, handled repossessions and drove the wrecker. Randy (as he was known by the locals) worked long hours but also made the most of sunny days at Lewes Beach, consorting with new friends.

One day, the tall, handsome southerner met a pretty local girl, Margaret "Peggy" Hastings, who worked in the billing office at the small local Beebe Hospital. They were introduced by Peggy's brother, Bobby, at the Gulf Gas Station Randy and Bobby frequented. Peggy was, above all else, funny: quick with a wisecrack, always laughing, never shy about speaking her mind and, when needed, putting someone in their place.

Peggy's grandparents owned a large farm outside town. Peggy lived with her mother on Third Street in the heart of Lewes where she could, and did, walk everywhere in town. When she was old enough, she babysat and worked at the Second Street five-and-ten. Apart from the winters, small-town life was wonderful.

As a teen, Peggy seldom lacked a date on weekends. Since her grandmother, her aunts and the Lewes mayor lived nearby and her house was directly behind the busy women's Zwanendael Club, it was hard for her to get into trouble. If she wasn't busy on a Friday or Saturday night, Peggy would take

Peggy Hastings's home behind the Zwanendael Club on Third Street. *Lewes Historical Society.*

a broom outside and sweep the sidewalk along Third Street. That was the signal for the boys cruising through town that Peggy was free to go out.

Randall took to her instantly, but Peggy already had a boyfriend. Peggy thought Randy was a "bumpkin" until she realized how smart and capable he actually was.

Britts (short for Brittingham's) was a popular restaurant in the High Victorian–style Scott Building on Second Street across from St. Peter's Church. The restaurant grill was kept sizzling from 7:00 a.m. to 11:00 p.m. for both locals and the scores of men who went out early and returned late on the menhaden fishing boats. No meal cost more than $1.50.

The owner, Emory Brittingham, was a former army MP and future Lewes police chief. Emory and his wife, Hazel (the babysitter for Captain Egan's twin girls), lived upstairs, in what had been a popular and proper gentleman's club, the Lewes Club, in the 1890s. All its members were required to don top hats when they were out on the town.

Britt's ice cream fountain was a popular hangout for local teens. Randy and Peggy began to meet there for shakes and burgers. Hazel Brittingham,

Brittingham's Restaurant

203 Second Street   Lewes, Delaware

Open From 7 A. M. to 12 Midnight

We Serve

BREAKFAST – LUNCH – SNACKS – DINNER

Full Course Dinners Served From 5 til 7 P. M.
At $1.00 to $1.50 – No Meals Over $1.50

Sea Food, Roast Beef, Chops, Steaks and Many Others

CHOICE OF 25 TASTY SANDWICHES
SPECIAL PRICES ON ALL LARGE ORDERS

Fountain Service – Ice Cream, Sodas, Sundaes, Cones
Orders Prepared "To Go"

"We Are the Largest Seller of Ice Cream"

VISIT OUR NEW RESTAURANT AND TRY OUR DELICIOUS SUBS
SMALL SUBS 25c — LARGE SUBS 45c

We Serve Abbotts' Dairies Ice Cream

Above: Britt's menu: "No meals over $1.50." *Hazel Brittingham.*

Left: Emory and Hazel Brittingham. Hazel would become Lewes's preeminent historian. *Hazel Brittingham.*

who would become Lewes's preeminent historian, recalls Randall as "funny, with a big personality." After a summer in Lewes, Randall returned to Georgia to attend a funeral. Then he enlisted with the coast guard at Cape May, New Jersey, visible on clear days across the Delaware Bay from Lewes.

Randall reunited with Peggy Hastings at a party in Lewes. The boyfriend was no longer in the picture. This time, their relationship took hold. The young couple spent days on Lewes Beach and went on long drives together.

Peggy and Randy on
Lewes Beach. *Amy Kreisler.*

They got married in 1953. Peggy's two favorite photos, kept at her bedside all her life, are of Randall with two pals on Lewes Beach and of herself on a beach towel, smiling happily. She positions the framed photos facing each other because, as she likes to remark, "It was me he was looking at."

With John Rollins's help, the young couple rented rooms in Isabel Jacob's Pilottown Road house and Preserve, "where the drain ran through," as Peggy recalled. Coincidentally, they spent their first ten months of married life at the same place where the Wiltbancks, Wests and others had lived centuries before them.

Randall worked off his commitment with the coast guard that year while he tried his hand at whatever new small-business opportunities seemed promising. Those included house painting, after-hours card games, pinball machines, reselling cars he bought at auction and working in the leasing business for his uncle John.

"Some things worked, others didn't. I did the taxes, if you can believe it," Peggy said. "That's how we learned."

ROLLINS REALTY BUYS THE PRESERVE

John Rollins, like Helms Wiltbanck centuries before, had his eye on the Preserve. Although Isabel refused to sell, she agreed to give him a first option to purchase the Preserve in her will. When Isabel died in 1956, John bought the thirty acres for $6,320, or $210.67 per acre, which was higher than its appraised value. This would be the first property acquired by the newly formed Rollins Realty. In its deed, the Preserve was described as being "80% in farm fields and the remainder forest," no doubt based on an earlier description during Captain Wingate's ownership. Soon it would be entirely forest again.

The second property Rollins Realty purchased was the 196-acre farm Peggy's grandparents owned outside Lewes. Randall sneaked his father out of Beebe Hospital, where he'd been in traction for his back, to the auction that was taking place in front of Sussex Trust, where they placed the winning bid. Wayne was soon raising cattle there as well as farming. Throughout his life, Wayne Rollins would buy more than seventy thousand acres of land across the United States and seldom sell any of it. Their love of land was something Wayne and Randall always shared.

WITH A LOAN FROM his uncle, Randall opened his own service station, which was profitable until the station manager embezzled its funds. He was suddenly over his head in debt—until Henry Tippie helped Randall consolidate his loans. After succeeding in every task his father and uncle threw at him, Randall became, essentially, the "fixer" for Rollins Inc. He excelled at broadcast sales and, at one critical point, rescued the company

The Preserve in 1954, two years before John Rollins's purchase. Isabel Jacob allowed a return to forest a decade earlier. *University of Delaware.*

from a disastrous investment in the billboard business that could have ruined them. Wayne rewarded him with the vice presidency of Rollins Outdoor Advertising. "If we told him we needed the Brooklyn Bridge," his uncle John said, "we'd turn around and see Randall floating that bridge down the river."

Rollins Broadcasting continued to expand its footprint, and in time, the young couple, by then with three children, relocated to Wilmington to be near the new Rollins Inc. headquarters.

THE ORKIN ADVENTURE

In 1964, acting on a tip from investment advisor George "Frolic" Weymouth from Chadd's Ford, Pennsylvania, Rollins Broadcasting looked into acquiring Orkin Pest Control in Atlanta, Georgia. It was a huge risk. Valued at $62.7 million, Orkin was many times larger than Rollins Broadcasting—and Wayne knew nothing of the pest control industry. Yet Orkin was profitable, if badly managed.

In the end, Wayne finalized the deal that year, using Orkin's own future stream of earnings as collateral for loans. Investment analysts described it as the first leveraged buyout in U.S. business history, earning Wayne a future place in the Wall Street Hall of Fame.

The two hundred Orkin branches with four thousand employees in twenty-nine states were operating with little oversight. To devote the time needed to his new company, Wayne assigned management of all the Rollins Broadcasting entities to Randall.

Only nine months after purchasing Orkin, the value of Rollins Inc. stock had more than tripled, from fifteen to fifty-two dollars per share. Wayne relocated his Rollins Inc. business entities from Wilmington to Georgia, and Randall and Peggy had to move again, this time far from Peggy's Lewes family and friends.

On his own, Randall found them a large but run-down house in north Atlanta, which he promised to sell soon. Peggy undertook a complete renovation, and as of this writing, the family has lived there for fifty-seven years.

Acquiring Orkin was a huge gamble; Wall Street bet on Rollins. *Amy Kreisler.*

FROM WILMINGTON TO JAMAICA

In the meantime, at the urging of legendary U.S. senator John J. Williams, a farmer from Millsboro, John Rollins ran for and was, surprisingly, elected lieutenant governor of Delaware, with voter support generated by the popularity of his down-home radio advertising. Unfortunately, Kitty didn't want the life of a politician's wife. She left John after the two of them had raised their four children at Tradewinds, their home on Lewes Beach.

From their first Rollins Inc. offices in Wilmington, John and Wayne had embarked on an ambitious plan to redevelop the downtown, which raised the ire of the embedded northern Delaware power structure and contributed to Wayne's decision to leave for Georgia after acquiring Orkin. John then built a fifteen-story Rollins Inc. office building on Concord Pike in Wilmington and bought a chateau in Greenville, both of which further alarmed the local elite. His creative plans to grow regional businesses were constantly challenged.

John was a colorful, natural salesman and a true visionary. His philosophy was to invest in eight to ten things and make a fortune from the two that succeeded. He got into the hazardous waste disposal business two decades before any other major players. He pioneered cable TV in Sussex County, then purchased Dover Downs harness racing for $1 million to help a friend. John had to invest $11 million more before slot machines and stock car racing made Dover Downs profitable.

After losing a bid to become Delaware's governor by five hundred votes and enduring years of having his Wilmington business efforts stymied, John turned his interests to Jamaica, an island nation he had come to love for its beauty and mysterious history. John invested heavily in Jamaica, buying and restoring Rose Hall, a deserted plantation with seven thousand acres stretching from a seven-mile beachfront to the mountains. Determined to increase the island's tourism, John also invested in a Holiday Inn with 550 rooms in Montego Bay and began planning for an Intercontinental Hotel.

Then, in the 1970s, the cost of borrowing began to climb. Within the decade, mortgage rates would rise to 12.9 percent and business loans to 18 percent. John, like many other entrepreneurs, was caught—in his case with interest payments alone costing him more than $1 million a month.

Henry Tippie, the Rollins accountant, was called back from his home in Texas to help. John gave him free rein to make the necessary cuts. After the dust settled, John was left with stock in Rollins Inc., his ownership of RLC Jamaica and his beloved Walnut Green chateau in Greenville. Also gone was his second wife, who had departed with her divorce attorney.

Left: John Rollins with his new bride, Michelle Metrinko. *Michelle Rollins.*

Below: Lifelong friends Johnny and June Cash becoming godparents to Michael Rollins. *Michelle Rollins.*

Opposite: President Nixon arrives at John Rollins's Greenville chateau, met by Governor Pierre duPont and Senators Robert Dole and William Roth. *Michelle Rollins.*

John soon rebounded and took a beautiful, young Ukrainian American attorney and former Miss USA World, Michele Metrinko, as his third wife. The couple's growing legion of friends ranged from President Richard Nixon to Texas governor John Connelly, Billy Graham and Duke Ellington, whom John may have met when the Duke performed at the Happy Day Club in Lewes in the early 1950s. John and Michele continued their focus on Jamaica for the next twenty-five years. They helped restore the Cinnamon Hill Great House for his lifelong friends Johnny and June Cash, who visited often and spent almost every New Year's Eve there with John and Michele for the next two decades.

Together, the Rollinses completed the Intercontinental, the Palms resort designed by Edward Durell and an authentic architectural restoration of the Rose Hall Great House, a landmark historic site. Late in life, John cut the ribbon at the Rose Hall Ritz-Carlton (now the Hyatt Ziva) and the White Witch Golf Course, having singlehandedly brought international tourism to Jamaica.

Over John's last fifteen years, he and Michele spent their summers where everything began: in Lewes at Tradewinds. They drove frequently past the Preserve, and John never failed to mention his pride in having bought it. In 2000, John died as he probably would have wished: at work in his office, while taking a nap. Michele has continued as chair of the thriving Rose Hall for the past twenty-four years with the support of her four children.

TRAGEDY AND TRIUMPH

By 1970, Peggy and Randall had raised six healthy children and experienced a string of incredibly good fortune, thanks primarily to common sense and hard work. Then tragedy struck.

Their pretty eldest daughter, Rita, was headstrong like Randall but secretly a favorite. As punishment for sneaking off to see a boy, Rita had been sent off for the weekend with her grandparents, Wayne and Grace, to their country home at Catoosa Springs—which really was no punishment at all. Rita was speaking on their telephone to a friend in Atlanta when a lightning storm burst. A bolt struck the transformer box outside the cabin, and she was electrocuted. Wayne found Rita and cradled her in his arms, but she was gone. It was sadly ironic that the line had been installed by a childhood friend of Wayne's who had neglected to mount a lightning rod on the pole. Wayne refused to file a lawsuit. Too much had been lost already. Randall and Peggy were devastated. The recent birth of Amy, then six months old, and the presence in their home of Pam, thirteen, helped them survive the blow.

Randall (*left*) and his brother Gary Rollins, behind their father, Wayne. *Amy Rollins.*

When Wayne named Randall chair and CEO in 1975, Rollins Inc. had a market value of $801 million. By 2017, under Randall's leadership, it was valued at $17 billion. Today, Rollins Inc. is a global corporation with more than thirty subsidiaries and a share value on the NYSE making it one of the United States' top one hundred companies.

BACK IN LEWES

The Rollins family took many vacations together, but one of their favorites—certainly Peggy's—was their annual return to Lewes for the July Fourth holiday, which began in 1981 with the purchase of their Lewes Beach house and has continued for forty-four years since.

Margaret Rollins loved being in her hometown, where her friends still knew the couple as Peggy and Randy. From their bayfront house, they could watch local fireworks on the beach, bicycle and walk to the nearby Dairy Queen and downtown.

At any time, there might be ten or forty family members there, including Michele, Uncle John and their children, who liked to stroll over from Tradewinds nearby. Randall especially enjoyed spending time with his uncle, who had always been his biggest fan, often just sitting together on the porch overlooking the bay.

Family members relaxing on the Rollinses' Lewes Beach house porch. *Amy Kreisler.*

The Preserve as seen from Fourth Street (toward Canary Creek). *Deny Howeth.*

Over time, the Rollinses maintained the 30 acres of the Preserve to remain as a forest. In 1987, for a token ten dollars, they gave the City of Lewes the right to extend Fourth Street across the Preserve to provide access to a new home community then being built, dividing it into 7 acres to the east of the road and 22.8 to the west.

As their wealth grew, Randall and Peggy formed a family foundation, Ma-Ran, which focused on health care and education in Georgia and, at their direction, gave substantial gifts to many Lewes charities, most notably Beebe Hospital, Lewes Library, Children's Beach House and, fittingly, the Lewes Historical Society and Museum.

Randall entertained periodic offers to sell and develop the Preserve but always rejected them. "He just didn't want to sell," Peggy said. Randall no doubt recalled his father's instruction about good property: never sell it unless you can use the money to buy better land. And what land could be better to own and protect than the very first acres purchased by Rollins Realty? It was land with sentimental value to Randall and Peggy in her small town, where Rollins Inc. got its start.

Plus, as it turned out, the Preserve is land with a priceless historic value.

CHANGE SWEEPS THROUGH LEWES

By 2015, the coastal region of Sussex County had become a magnet for baby boom retirees due to its low taxes, temperate climate and, at the time, affordable home prices. Of all the Sussex communities, Lewes was the most sought after.

Local and national developers seized the opportunity, buying up virtually all the surrounding farmland as well as any available open space within city limits. Most of the modest houses in Lewes's traditional African American neighborhoods were quickly acquired and taken down. Other descendants of older Lewes families chose to cash out rather than retain their ancestral homes, many of which needed repair. Thanks to the foresight of the City of Lewes, homes in the historic district could be remodeled but not removed.

Soon it became difficult for Peggy to orient herself during summer visits, so sweeping were the changes to the landscape. What's more, while the city's population stayed the same, the population around Lewes had exploded.

Most of the new residents now live in upscale developments tightly encircling the city in homes worth well over $1.5 million. The value of lots and houses in town has tripled in value. Thousands of well-off baby boom retirees and remote workers suddenly want to live in the small, close-knit community—and in the process, Lewes is being changed forever.

ONE MEMORABLE WEEK IN 2017, many of the Rollins clan, children and grandchildren, came to Lewes to see what the small city meant to Randall and Peggy and vice versa. The occasion was the opening of the Margaret Rollins Community Center and Lewes History Museum.

Her family called it "the tour." As she did with everyone on their first visit to Lewes, Peggy drove them around to see where her family farm had been, her old home on Third Street and 360 Pilottown at the Preserve, Peggy and Randall's first stop as a married couple.

At seventy-eight, Randall had survived a devastating cancer diagnosis by undergoing more than a year of treatment many men his age could not have withstood. He was tired that week, but Randall still participated in every event. Everywhere they walked, he and Peggy held hands.

To anyone he had just met who didn't know him as one of the country's wealthiest and most successful business leaders, Randall would say, "I'm just a farmer."

Randall lived three more years until passing away in 2020, celebrating each July Fourth in Lewes with Peggy and their family around him.

After Randall's death, Peggy began to spend entire summers at their Lewes Beach house. In 2022, she contacted the Greater Lewes Foundation with an option to buy the Preserve and permanently protect it. Because her large family was inheriting and selling much of Randall's land, Peggy purchased the Preserve at its appraised value of $11.4 million from the family, then placed the Preserve in a new trust with a discounted price of $8 million. At this writing, the GLF has raised 50 percent of that amount with the help of more than one thousand Lewes donors.

Margaret and Randall Rollins.
Amy Kreisler.

THE GIVING LAND

Like the fabled giving tree, the Preserve gave of itself to support the dreams, livelihoods and prosperity of generations of Lewes residents.

After 355 years, the Preserve is still alive, home to a thriving habitat of deer, wild turkeys, birds (including two bald eagles), amphibians and fragile native plants. Its hundreds of trees provide a canopy of shade that helps cool the local environment and calls out to be walked beneath. It is our last forest, the living, beating heart of Lewes.

After the Preserve is acquired, it will be owned by the City of Lewes under a conservation easement allowing only natural walking trails. A separate master plan will ensure the Preserve's future prosperity: its groundwater will be managed by strategically placed wetland ponds and its forest replenished with native species of plants and trees.

The master plan will encourage educational use. Students will be able to walk from nearby schools to study ecology and history in a real-life natural laboratory. Educators from the Cape District and the Lewes campus of the University of Delaware College of Earth, Ocean and Environment are being encouraged to incorporate the Preserve for field trips and studies in their curricula.

The Preserve will provide a doorway to Lewes's past, where everyone can walk among tall, swaying trees and scented underbrush and be transported 350 years, back to Lewes's earliest days, when Helms Wiltbanck stood there, hands on his hips, thinking about his future.

And now ours.

> *I took a walk in the woods and came out taller than the trees.*
> —*Henry David Thoreau*

For more information about the Fourth Street Preserve campaign, please visit osalewes.org and the Greater Lewes Foundation website, greaterlewesfoundation.org. Calls are welcomed at (302) 644-0107.

Tax deductible donations to the campaign can be made online or mailed c/o the GLF at 135 Second Street, Lewes, Delaware 19958.

ACKNOWLEDGEMENTS

S o many people have assisted with this book. Dr. Edward Otter, Lewes's premier archaeological historian, was generous with his knowledge and advice, and Dr. Heidi Nasstrom Evans, director of the Rehoboth Beach History Museum, first brought my attention to the historic importance of the Preserve.

A special thanks to Margaret "Peggy" Rollins for sharing her reminiscences of Lewes and her life with Randall Rollins and to her daughter, Amy Kreisler, president of the Ma-Ran Foundation, for patiently reviewing my writing about her amazing family. Appreciation is also due Michele Rollins for taking time from her work at Rose Hall in Jamaica to correct and fill in many important details about her life with John Rollins.

Longtime Lewes friends shared their memories, including Doris Ingram, longtime owner of the Egan house on Pilottown Road; Nick Carter; Chris Nibour; and Hazel Brittingham, legendary Lewes historian, whose name graces the archives at the Lewes Historical Society.

Deny Howeth, Lewes photographer, and Ray Daminger, our graphic designer, supported this project with top-quality professional services. Gary and Betty Grunder provided superb editing advice. My friend and colleague Paul Sparrow donated hours tracking the history of the West family.

Sincere thanks to the authors credited in the bibliography, many of them personal friends, whose own research and stories in *Journal of the Lewes Historical Society* added tremendously to this book. Also, deep appreciation to Denise Clemons, chair of the LHS, who granted me off-hour access to the

Sally Freeman Research Room and permission for the use of information and illustrations from the museum's archives, collections and journals.

I benefited greatly from the encouragement of my colleagues at the Greater Lewes Foundation, notably Joe Stewart, Hugh Leahy and Jim Ford, who championed this project from the start. And lastly, thanks to new friends, Kate Jenkins, acquisitions editor at The History Press, for her encouragement and patient guidance and to Zoe Ames, the book's fine copyeditor.

SELECTED BIBLIOGRAPHY

Archdeacon, Herbert. "All Aboard! The Trains to Lewes." *Journal of the Lewes Historical Society* 1 (December 1998).

Beers, D.G. Map of Lewes and Rehoboth Beach. 1868.

Cohen, William J. *Swanendael in New Netherland: The Early History of Delaware's Oldest Settlement at Lewes.* Lewes, DE: Lewes Historical Society, 2004.

Colonial National Park Service. "The Dust of Many a Hard-Fought Field." National Park Foundation, April 6, 2022.

Cullen, Virginia. *History of Lewes, Delaware.* Lewes, DE: Col. David Hall Chapter, Daughters of the American Revolution, 1981.

Deeb, Susan. *Triple R: The Life of R. Randall Rollins.* Atlanta, GA: Self-published, 2018.

Delaware AHGP. "Town of Lewes, Lewes and Rehoboth Hundred." American History and Genealogy Project, n.d.

Delaware Environmental Monitoring & Analysis Center. Delaware Geological Survey. Aerial photographs courtesy University of Delaware.

De Valinger, Leon Jr. "The Burning of the Whorekil, 1673." *Pennsylvania Magazine of History and Biography* 74, no. 4 (1950).

Dipaolo, Michael. "The Early Plank House." *Journal of the Lewes Historical Society* 5 (November 2002).

Ferris, Benjamin. *A History of the Original Settlements on the Delaware.* Self-published, August 1865.

Gehron, William J. "Historical Vignettes In & About Lewes." CALRA Free Press newsletter, 2011.

General Assembly of the State of Delaware, Duke of York Records 1646–1679. Wilmington, DE: Sunday Star Print, 1899.

Haden, Amy. *Victorian Lewes and Its Architecture.* Lewes, DE: Lewes Historical Society and the Preservation Trust, 1986.

Hancock, Harold B. "Not Quite Men: The Free Negroes in Delaware in the 1830s." *Civil War History* 17, no. 4 (December 1971).

Herndon, John Goodwin. "Wiltbanks of Sussex Co DE, PA." *Genealogical Magazine* 17, no 1 (December 1950).

Holland, Randy J. *Delaware's Destiny Determined by Lewes.* Dover, DE: Delaware Heritage Commission, 2013.

Hollaway, Paula Schwartz. "Robert West Mustard: An American Merchant in Shanghai." *Delaware History* 2 (Spring–Summer 1986).

Hugg, David. "Lewes: Center for Education." *Delaware Coast Press*, April 29, 1971.

Hunt, Brian, "Lt. Abraham Wiltbank, Patriot of Lewes, Forgotten Patriots," July 19, 2024

Knopp, Andrew. *One Hundred Year History of the Pilots' Association, 1896–1996.* Dover, DE: Delaware Heritage Press, May 1996.

Kotowski, Bob. "Slavery and Politics." *Journal of the Lewes Historical Society* 21 (2018).

MacDonald, Warren. "The Duke of York Patents on Pilottown Road." *Journal of the Lewes Historical Society* 5 (November 2002).

Manthorpe, William. "The Battle to Control the Delaware Assembly." *Journal of the Lewes Historical Society* 23, 2020.

Margaret Rollins Community Center and Lewes History Museum. Family History Collections: Ingram, Mustard, West, Wiltbanck.

Marine, David. "Duke of York Patents on Pilot Town Road." *The Archeolog* 7, no. 2 (September 1955).

Marvill, James E., ed. *A Pictorial History of Lewes, Delaware, 1609–1985.* Lewes, DE: Lewes Historical Society, 1985.

McIlvaine, George Marshall. Town of Lewes Map, 1890–1900 *Journal of the Lewes Historical Society* 5 (November 2002).

Moore, J. Everett, Jr. *Growin' Up Country: Rural Life in the 1950s and 1960s.* Georgetown, DE: Springfield Historic Preservation, 2012.

Moore, Kevin N. *Lewes, Delaware: Celebrating 375 Years of History.* Lewes, DE: MM Publishing, 2006.

Morgan, Michael. *Hidden History of Lewes.* The History Press, Charleston, SC: 2014.

Morning News. "Judge Wiltbank Helped Found State, Served in War." July 9, 1965.

Munroe, John A. *Colonial Delaware: A History.* Dover, DE: Delaware Heritage Press, 2003.

Orr, Robert Hunter. *A Small-Town Boyhood in the First State.* Lewes, DE: Sassafras Press, 1999, rev. 2001.

Otter, Edward. *St. George's AME Cemetery on Pilottown Road, Lewes, Delaware.* Project report to the Greater Lewes Foundation, Lewes, DE, August 31, 2021.

Patience, Essah. *Slavery and Freedom in the First State.* Los Angeles: University of California, 1985.

Pifer, Barry. *Hanging the Moon: The Rollins Rise to Riches.* Newark: University of Delaware Press, 1951.

Roberts, Judith Atkins. "The Hiram Burton House." *Journal of the Lewes Historical Society* 8 (November 1999).

Rogers, Steve, and Bob Kotowski. "Boat Building in Lewes." *Journal of the Lewes Historical Society* 15 (November 2012).

Ruth, Jim. "Land Ho: Pennsylvania Merchant Arrives at Lewes." *Lewes History* 26 (July 2023).

Society of the Cincinnati. *Delaware in the American Revolution: An Exhibition.* Anderson House, Washington, D.C., October 12, 2002.

Stewart, Robert, "Ancient Stone Marker." *Journal of the Lewes Historical Society* 8 (November 1999).

Stone, Letta Broek. "The West Family Register." Lewes History Museum records.

Terrell, Dan. *Eight Flags Over Lewes.* Rehoboth Beach, DE: Duck Press, 1975.

Weslanger, Clinton Alfred. *Dutch Explorers, Traders, and Settlers in the Delaware Valley, 1609–1664.* Philadelphia: University of Pennsylvania Press, 1961.

———. *The Siconese Indians of Lewes, Delaware.* Lewes, DE: Lewes Historical Society, 1991.

Wilmington Evening Journal. "Brother Mustard's Orthodoxy." July 20, 1898.

Wray, Gary. *Fort Miles.* Charleston, SC: Arcadia Publishing, 2005.

INDEX

ABOUT THE AUTHOR

Michael Rawl developed his writing skills at the *Washington Daily News* and then with PR and advertising firms in Washington, D.C. He became director of marketing for *The Source*, a Reader's Digest company, and later director of marketing communications for Entré Computer and VP of investor relations and corporate giving for Intelligent Electronics. Rawl spent the rest of his career as president of community foundations for Chester County, Pennsylvania, and the Chesapeake Bay region before founding Horizon Philanthropic Services, a Delaware consulting firm for nonprofit organizations, and the Greater Lewes Foundation in 2000. He is the author of *Anacostia Flats*, the story of the Bonus Marchers in Washington, D.C. Rawl and his wife, Mary, have lived and worked in Lewes, Delaware, for the past thirty-seven years.

Visit us at
www.historypress.com